rhythm paul d science miller

AKA DJ SPOOKY THAT SUBLIMINAL KID.

EDITORIAL DIRECTOR
PETER LUNENFELD

DESIGN
COMA AMSTERDAM/NEW YORK

MEDIAWORK/THE MIT PRESS
CAMBRIDGE, MASSACHUSETTS
LONDON, ENGLAND

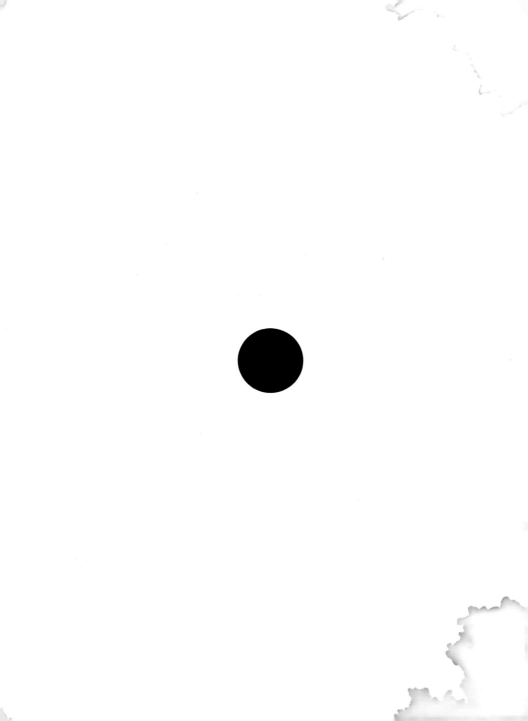

a-side

THE IDIOT – A FREESTYLE

THE IDIOT – A FREESTYLE

The beginning. That's always the hard part. Once you get into the flow of things, you're always haunted by the way that things could have turned out. This outcome, that conclusion. You get my drift. The uncertainty is what holds the story together, and that's what I'm going to talk about. Rhythm Science. Myth Science. A catalog of undecided moments at the edge of my thinking process. This is not about pseudonyms or alter egos. That's already been done. Think of this book as an exploration of the cold logic of the surface. Ice: Ice isn't just ice in this picture; it's ice cubed, the "changing same" bounced against itself on the cold surfaces people create when they

name themselves, cool as Kool. Make the link between the names people make up, and the image resolves. The game face moves from version to version. Whether you're logging in under a new name, or you're a Dj trying out a new persona, the logic is an extension rather than a negation. Alias, a.k.a.; the names describe a process of loops. From A to B and back again. Dig beneath what lies on the surface only to arrive where you started. It's a circular logic, a database logic. Surface meets surface in a translation game of chilled desire.

Rhythm science is not about "transparency" of intent. Rhythm science is a forensic investigation of sound as a vector of a coded language that goes from the physical to the informational and back again. Rhythm science. Rhyme time. Rough trade. Sound. Think of it as a mirror held up to a culture that has learned to fly again, that has released itself from the constraints of the ground to drift through dataspace, continuously morphing its form in response to diverse streams of information. Sound is a product of many different editing environments, an end result of an interface architecture that twists and turns in sequences overlaid with slogans, statistics, vectors, labels, and grids.

Sound. Think of it as a dance of neologisms, an anemic cinema for the gene-splice generation where sign and symbol, word and meaning all drift into the sonic maelstrom. This is a world where all meaning has been untethered from the ground of its origins and all signposts point to a road that you make up as you travel through the text. Rotate, reconfigure, edit, render the form. Contemporary sound composition

is an involution engine. Traditional drawings and models have given way to animations, scans, and readouts, and sound has become a digital signifier whose form adjusts its shape in front of us like an amorphous cloud made of zeros and ones, 1s and 0s.

The beginning. That's always the hard part. Once you get into the flow of things, you're always haunted by the way that things could have turned out. This outcome, that conclusion. You get my drift.

The term "vector" comes from geometry and refers to a line of fixed length and direction but no fixed position. Consider the way ideas move through our minds and bodies. There is no fixed position. There's only the improvisational nature of recall. Thought vector: the relationship between a geometry and a geography of information. Sound vector: think lines of flight in the digital now. Vector of a sound in motion: wave propagation and particles of thought. The mean machine of how we perceive language floats across the scenario, its

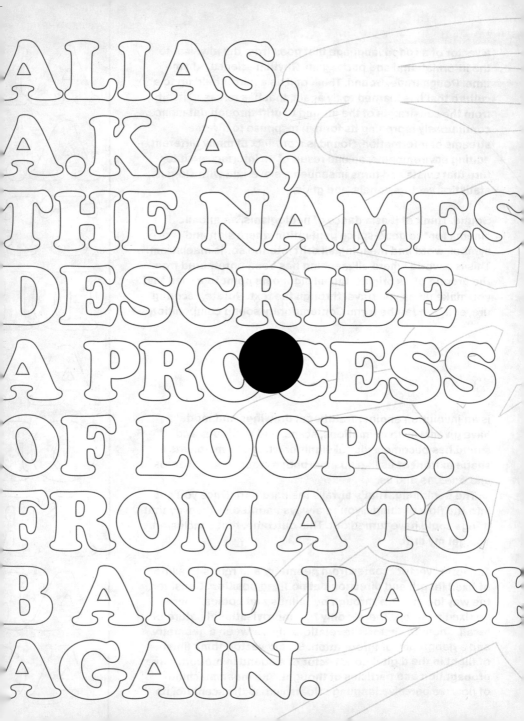

ALIAS, A.K.A.; THE NAMES DESCRIBE A PROCESS OF LOOPS. FROM A TO B AND BACK AGAIN.

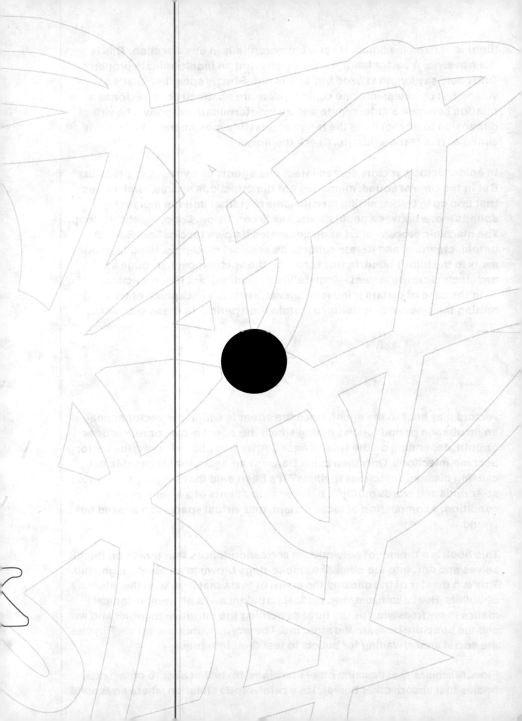

flight is of fixed maximum length, but potentially in any direction. This is the freestyle. A vector has a fixed property and an indeterminate property. One could say length is fixed but axis is not. Strictly speaking, that's a vector. But by extension, one could think more abstractly of a vector as a relation between a determinate and an indeterminate property. The virtual dimension to any vector is the range of possible movements of which it is capable. This is the wildstyle. Check the flow.

In epidemiology, vectors spread infectious agents like viruses or parasites But in the case of sound, memories are the infectious spores, viral modes that pop up in tracks, sifting mechanisms that filter and file memory as sounds move between populations. Sex is confusion. Loop, repetition, loop. The machinic process of creation generates its own fascination. Sounds unfold, organize, and iterate cultures as abstract machines, filing memories away in the idiot's mind. In this scenario, the vector moves through an architectonic environment – form follows function, fact follows fiction.
    In the case of certain infectious agents, vectors are capable of trans-mitting the disease only during a certain time period. In these situations,

vectors play host to the agent. Once the agent is within the vector animal, an incubation period follows during which the agent grows or reproduces or both, depending on the type of agent. After this phase is over, the vector become infectious. Only then can it transmit an agent that is capable of causing disease. Infectious rhythms? It's been said that language is a virus, so sounds and words multiply, become viral agents of an omni-sensory condition, a compilation of local, distant, and virtual spaces, all evoked by sound.

This book is a theater of networks, of correspondences that turn in on them-selves and drift into the ether like smoke-rings blown in an airless nightclub. This is a theater of the one and the many, of texts that flow with the intensity of bullets. Heat death, entropy, cyclical turbulence. It's all here. Technical malice in my freestyle rips the threads holding the narrative together and we see the structure beneath the structure. The words within the words. Rhymes are social armor, waiting for bullets to test their integrity.

Flow. Machines that describe other machines, texts that absorb other texts, bodies that absorb other bodies. It's a carnivorous situation where any sound can be you, and where any word you say is already known. Flow, counter-flow. The idiot as processing device, slave to the moment, outside of time because for him there is only the moment of thought. No past, no present, no future. The idiot is a zombie, a character straight out of *Thriller*, one of Michael Jackson's chorus line of decaying bodies moving into y'all's neighborhood. Watch the idiots dance to rhythms they do not feel or understand. There is our beginning, and there is our narrative path. The person without qualities who cannot say "I." The person whom others speak through, who has no central identity save what he or she knows. And what they know is that they know there is nothing else. That is the narrative role of the idiot in this journey, and that is where I begin this scenario.

So as we flow across the page in the here and now, and as you process the words as you read them, remember this: They process you as well. Roam the interstices of globalization as a ghost in the machine as we fast-forward past the middle passage and into the hyperlinks of a database culture whose archives routed and dissolved into almost every format of memory we've thought about, and think about how to describe the experience. Is it as simple as flipping open a laptop and joining a wireless network? Is it as automatic as dialing a phone number on

Check t

a mobile phone in an unfamiliar city? Home is where your cell phone is. An absurd reductionist logic? Plastic, fluid memories run into circuitry and focus our attention on a world where we download ourselves daily. This is a word game of the nonconscious. This is what the idiot tells us, and this is what we reply.

There's always more than one map to the territory: You just have to intuit the terrain. Why do you like the sounds of electronic music? Because you need to. Because there's a relentless progression from need to act, from gesture and thought, to that machinic cultural conditioning. Input, output. The sequence is tight. The loops are relentless. Play your hand, find out what the dealer deals. The rest is the remix. Unpack the meanings, unstuff the fragments and the logic remains the same: the part speaks for the whole, the whole is an extension of the part. It's a holographic thing. As George Santayana said so long ago, "Those who cannot remember the past are condemned to repeat it." That's one scenario. But what happens when the memories filter through the machines we use to process culture and become software – a constantly updated, always turbulent terrain more powerful than the machine through which it runs? Memory, damnation, and repetition: That was then, this is now. We have machines to repeat history for us. And the software that runs the machines is the text that flows through the

the flow.

conduits like a *flaneur* of the unconscious. These are tales told over and over so many times and in so many ways that the texts undergo rigor mortis while they hum with the speed of a thousand and one nights. Murmur to yourself and hear the voices in your head whisper back. That's the logic. Press "return." Process. It's a tale of constant change unto itself. The circuitry of the machines is the constant in this picture; the software is the embodiment of infinite adaptability, an architecture of frozen music, unthawed. Watch the flow: That's the content versus context scenario of Dj culture. Hardware, wetware, shareware, software: The invisible machinery of the codes that filter the sounds is omnivorous.

Opposites extract.

ALSO KNOWN AS

"Dj Spooky is one of those cats you just see everywhere. He's at a dinner party in NYC one night, the next he's doing a show at London's ICA on new software and music on the internet, and yet the next night, he's in Tokyo doing a show with, oh, I don't know, Dj Krush or something... Basically he's a Dj who doesn't really fit into the normal roles of a beat master. He's a Dj with a lot of information and people streaming through his mind. We thought we'd just tap the flow for a bit, and see what downloads."

– From a three-way interview between Ad Astra (an alias), Dj Spooky (another persona), and Paul D. Miller (who created them both).

"Dj Spooky that Subliminal Kid" is a living engagement with an ultra media-saturated youth culture. Creating this identity allowed me to spin narratives on several fronts at the same time and to produce persona as shareware. I started Dj-ing as a conceptual art project, but as the Spooky persona took on a life of its own, I came to regard it as a social sculpture, coding a generative syntax for new languages of creativity. "Spooky" grew from the fact that the disembodied music I loved – hip-hop, techno, ambient, futurjazz, spacedub – was itself a syntactic space reflecting the world I knew. This strange "beatless" music embodied the central talismans of consensual reality; its spooky, displaced sounds represented the space between dreams. The latter part of this alias, "that Subliminal Kid," comes from William S. Burroughs' darkly absurd sci-fi novel, *Nova Express*. The Subliminal Kid is battling the deadly Nova Mob, which is trying to take over Earth's mind screens and send out hate signals. The Subliminal Kid breaks into the Reality Studio and fights the Mob by manipulating tape loops, hoping that if the association lines holding the past and present together are ruptured, the future will leak through.

Another inspiration, or weird hero if you prefer, is the Victorian era biologist, Paul Kammerer. He was the first person to really explore ideas of synchronicity: the ways in which things, actions, and events converge in time. Kammerer would

THE METHOD BECOM
"ACTIONARY" RATHE
THAN "RE-ACTIONAR

move through his environment collecting examples of simultaneity, marking and registering coincidences with mathematical precision. He searched long and hard for an equation that would describe how things manifested in urban reality, a "law of series or sequences" (which parallels, of course, how we refer to the elements of a music track these days). Kammerer was looking for the algorithms of everyday life – how patterns appear, and how their structures can affect all aspects of the creative act. In other words, patterns ain't just about bein' digital. They are global. They are universal. There are rhythms that hold everything we know and can understand together. Kammerer's idea of sequential reality and process-oriented events was one of the first systematic attempts at figuring out a rhythm of everyday life in an industrial context. These kinds of investigations aren't easy, and Kammerer's ended badly: he committed suicide. But I'm more concerned with praxis – how to foster a milieu where dialog about culture becomes a way to move into the pictures we describe with words, text, sounds – you name it.

The method becomes "actionary" rather than "re-actionary" – you end up with a culture that is healthier and more dynamic. What Kammerer would call a series, someone like Henry Louis Gates would call "signifyin." It's all about how we play

THE METHOD BECOMES "ACTIONARY" RATHER THAN "RE-ACTIONARY"

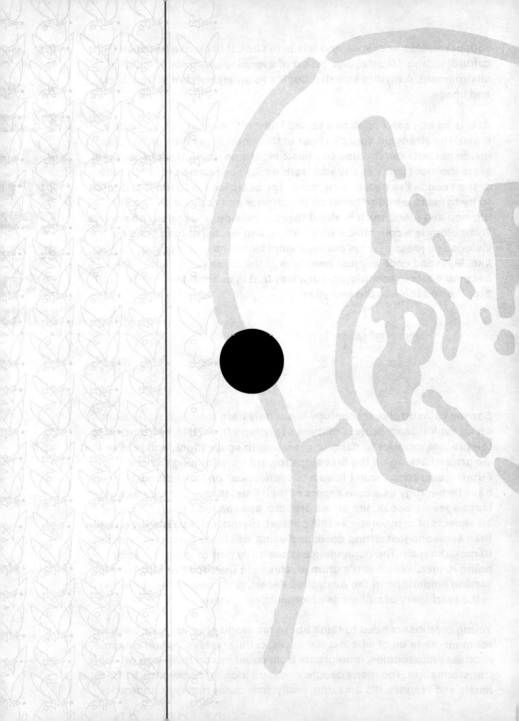

with perception of events, and this is the link that I make between Dj culture, techno-science, and the art of everyday creativity in a digital environment. A rhythm scientist begins as an archivist of sound, text, and image.

At this point, I can't think of a sound I haven't heard or that I couldn't make. The strangest sounds I hear at this point in my life come from inside not outside. Dreams and basic nighttime thought processes generate the most creative sounds. Nothing else can come close to some of the sounds I've heard in my mind. The basic idea is to use the digital to try to make a bridge between the interior and exterior. Music like hip-hop and electronica is about theater: how people live to the sounds. Technology is a collective hallucination, and we are able to send our visions and ideas in ways our ancestors would have thought were god-like. Myth and code are just two sides of the same coin; people are becoming more technological in a way that is at heart how we live and breathe and think in the everyday.

Barring catastrophe, technology is not only here to stay, it now exists on an evolutionary scale. Combine everything from DNA sequencing to telepresent robotics to nano-engineering to space flight, and realize that we are embarking on the first steps toward transforming the species. Future generations won't have a "dependence" on technology. They will have technology as a core aspect of their existence – as much as the languages we speak, the air we breathe, and the food that we eat are all aspects of technology. In this context, rhythm science is a lot broader than someone just sitting down and using whatever computer is around to make sounds. The dependence is basically part of the process of being human. Whether it's drum machines in the Bronx or aboriginals playing didgeridoo in the Australian desert, what holds them together is the machinery of culture as an organizing system.

Young composers need to think about the world around them, an environment made up of wireless networks, cellular relays, hybrid systems, rootless philosophies, immigrants from countries on the verge of transformation. Too many people continue looking backwards to 12-tone music and Wagner. It's amazing, really, how many movie soundtracks

sound like heavy-handed treatments of *The Ring Cycle*'s overtures. The funda-
mental concepts of new music technology are just as much a part of this world
as PDAs or laptop computers. In industrialized countries, children come to understand video games, how to use cellphones, and how to navigate their urban and
suburban superstructures. They aren't alienated from these technological and
geographical phenomenon, they are born into them.

Humans have a certain perceptual architecture. The basic structure is the basilar
membrane of the ear. The sense of gravity and balance that we have comes from
there, and the frequencies that we can or cannot respond to come from there,
too. Beyond that, I've always been an optimist – I don't think we've engaged how
much we can hear. We're conditioned to accept the social ramifications of the
various technologies as constants in the environment, but they're as open to
fluctuation as the societies that generated them. All of which points to the fact
that it's not so much new ways of hearing that are needed, but new perceptions
of what we can hear.

The same track? The same beat? Day after day, night after night... it would be like

some kind of living death if that were to happen in Dj culture. Unfortunately,
that's how much of the culture works. But there are those – from Jamaican dub
artists to Silicon Valley engineers – who want to counter this entropy. They
propagate what Amiri Baraka called "the changing same": offering iterations of
versions and versions of everything, all change all the time. Inertia – it's not just
boring, it's against the basic principles of physics!

In 1960s Paris, the Situationists initiated concepts like the *dérive* or psychogeography, but these days that sense of wandering through an indeterminate
maze of intentionality can become the totality of the creative act. Selection,
detection, defining morphologies, and building structures, that's what make the
new art go round. The challenge is to keep striving to create new worlds, new
scenarios at almost every moment of thought, to float in an ocean of possibility.
The Dj "mix" is another form of text and its involutions, elliptical recursive qualities and repetitions are helping transform an "analog" literature into one that
is increasingly digitized. Dj-ing lets you take the best of what's out there and
give your own take on it. It's been said that science fiction is the literature of
alienation, a genre for those who don't relate to the world as it currently stands,
for those who want to create alternative zones of expression. Dj-ing for me, like

Dreams and basic nighttime thought processes generate the most creative sounds.

science fiction, points us to a place where every-thing doesn't have to be the same.

Life is interesting. The writing that gives meaning and some kind of hope to life in this world should be interesting as well. People really don't think about the absolute wonders that surround us and make this life livable and our way of thinking sustainable. Rhythm science creates parallel sound-scapes because it's music that says, "there could be another way." Rhythm science makes possible a music of permutation that tries to convey a sense of how conceptual art, contemporary technology, and timeless idealism might function together today.

THE NEW GRIOTS

The Dj crafts the physical form around an idea. Start with the inspiration of George Herriman's *Krazy Kat* comic strip. Make a track evoking his absurd land-scapes. Determine the atmospheric flows of wind. What do tons and tons of air pressure moving in the atmosphere sound like? Make music that acts as a metaphor for that kind of immersion or density. Visualize soundscapes; create imaginary projec-tions. The rhythm scientist proves there's more at work, more in the process, than the computerized musical automaton. At the end of the day, when you press PLAY on the CD, you don't necessarily care what the Dj was thinking about. You're just going to see if you like it or not. Without imagination, everything is empty. There are so many ways to drive each sequence, each track, each song.

Music is always a metaphor. It's an open signifier, an invisible, utterly malleable material. It's not fixed or cast in stone. Rhythm science uses an endless recontextualizing as a core compositional strategy, and some of this generation's most important artists continually remind us that there are innumerable ways to arrange the mix. The most innovative jump around genre definitions and styles at the flip of a hat rather than sticking to the same vernacular all their life. But too many others awash in the Great Sea of Pop Culture keep cranking out the same style over and over, working within restricted markets, genres, and styles. Electronic music makers, perhaps because they have access to so many different cultural products as raw material, are more willing to create psychological collage space.

The best Djs are griots, and whether their stories are conscious or unconscious, narratives are implicit in the sampling idea. Every story leads to another story to another story to another story. But at the same time, they might be called "music before the impact of language," or pre-linguistic stories. Core myths from the binary opposition at the center of the human mind. In the twenty-first century, stories disappear and evaporate as soon as they're heard, a sonic and cultural entropy. Mass counterbalances rhythm science's entropic drift, though, as the physical density of information becomes a new field open for interpretation.

Mass as a quality becomes an abstraction of the human environment, emblematic of hyper-commodification. Walk into a record store, look around, and there's so much shit that your memory just implodes. Move two blocks down to the bookstore, and there are dozens of new books a day. It's life in the data-cloud, of course, but it's also about life in a such a dense place that the human mind acts as kind of an osmotic unit, absorbing randomly but at the same time with some sort of underlying structure.

A deep sense of fragmentation occurs in the mind of a Dj. When I came to Dj-ing, my surroundings – the dense spectrum of media grounded in advanced capitalism – seemed to have already constructed so many of my aspirations and desires for me; I felt like my nerves extended to all of these images, sounds, other people – that all of them were extensions of myself, just as I was an extension of them. Trains, planes, automobiles, people, transnational corporations, monitor screens – large and small, human and non-human – all of these represent a seamless convergence of time and space in a world of compartmentalized moments and discrete invisible transactions. Somehow it all just works. Frames per second, pixels per square inch, color depth resolution measured in the millions of subtle combinations possible on a monitor screen… all of these media

Visualize soundscapes soundscapes

representations still need a designated driver. From the construction of time in a world of images and advertising, it's not that big a leap to arrive at the place the Wu-Tang Clan described in their song, "C.R.E.A.M" – "Cash Rules Everything Around Me." That's the end result of the logic of capitalist media's representations redux. Jean Baudrillard observes: "In spite of himself, the schizophrenic is open to everything and lives in the most extreme confusion. The schizophrenic is not, as generally claimed, characterized by the loss of touch with reality, but by the absolute proximity to and total instantaneousness with things [by] overexposure to the transparency of the world." By creating an analogical structure of sounds based on collage, with myself as the only common denominator, the sounds come to represent me.

No matter how much I travel, how much the global nomad, the troubadour, or the bard I become, this sonic collage becomes my identity. Blues musicians speak of "going to the crossroads" – that space where everyone could play the same song but flipped it every which way until it became "their own sound." In jazz, it's the fluid process of "call and response" between the players of an ensemble. These are the predecessors of the mixing board metaphor for how we live and think in

this age of information. The web is the dominant metaphor for the way we think. It is a living network made up of the "threads" of all the information moving through the world at any given moment. This emphasis on mobility creates a continuity between the techno-hype for the internet and everything from the nineteenth-century's obsession with railroads to the Beatnik's mythological automobiles on the road. Information and beats and rhythms never stay in one place. It's all about algorithms: code is beats is rhythm is algorithm is digital. Precedents for thinking about Dj culture are out there, especially if you're open to different interpretations of art and process. The problem is that no matter how intuitive this might sound, people still tend to be mad conservative when it comes to looking at things in a different light. But at the end of the day, the music speaks louder than any individual voice, and the music is saying that the old boundaries no longer exist. The present moment has been deleted. Any sound can be you: that's the idea of the nomad idea. Sound and signification: This is the electromagnetic situation.

"Dj tools" – stuff that people are meant to mix, and the technologies to do it – become important, but they have to leave enough room for people to check them out in their own way. Each and every Dj is a walking radio station transmitting his

own style. You just have to be open to
different frequencies. That's what makes
a good party; when there's different shit
going on, not just the same music all night.

It's the twenty-first century. Things should
be really wild. Anything else is boring.

code is beats is rhyth

SONIC SCULPTURES

Sampling is a new way of doing something
that's been with us for a long time: creating
with found objects. The rotation gets thick.
The constraints get thin. The mix breaks free
of the old associations. New contexts form
from old. The script gets flipped. The languages evolve and learn to speak in new
forms, new thoughts. The sound of thought
becomes legible again at the edge of the new
meanings. After all, you have to learn a new
language. Take the idea and fold it in on itself.
Think of it as laptop jazz, cybernetic jazz,
nu-bop, ILLbient – a nameless, formless,
shapeless concept given structure by the
rhythms. And that's a good start.

Sound and image divorce and reconfigure
before they reunite in the mix. The wheels turn,
the discs spin, the hard drives flow with the

igital. code is beats is rhythm

is algorithm is digital. code is

recursive logic of the tyranny of the beat. The times change and the music evolves. It's a stream of consciousness thing… But at the end of the day, it's all about the changing same, the core of repetition at modern thought. The samples and fragments speak the unspoken, the ascent remains unbroken. Nu-bop, nu-forms, nu-soundz: Flip the script, open the equation, check the situation. Guy Debord used to call this style detournement, Sigmund Freud called it the uncanny – we call it wildstyle. We call it carnival. We call it parade. And it's a way of life that's here to stay. It was all about situations then, and it's like that now, only a little more entrenched. Is it live? Or is it a sample? After almost three decades of rhythm science, the question remains just as powerful as ever. The uncanny remains with us. In the bebop era, Charlie Parker played notes from an underground that were about content rather than context. Today, the music of the invisible machine comes to us from our software: MAX/MSP, TRAKTOR, SUPERCOLLIDER, NATO 55, REASON, REBIRTH, RECYCLE, MIXMAN – the names and platforms go on, but the picture emerges. Software is infinite. Sonar is about the reflection of sound to ground us in an electronic environment. Think of bats flying in the night. Navigate the metaphor, cut and paste it into the here and now. *Commedia del arte* becomes digital, becomes total theater, becomes electronic. Feel the frequencies.

Rhythm science isn't just about sound, of course. Imagery, whether presented on canvas or seen as a series of repeated photographic, cinematic, televisual, or digitized stills has a way of evoking a "kinedramatic" imaginal response. Sometimes the images carve out a blank space that memory later gives meaning to. At other moments, they have an immediate, visceral effect. Angles of incidence leave paths of thought unresolved, a high-resolution photo frame-capture, still life, *nature-morte.* The technologies of rhythm science are an extension of what had long been going on. Computer interfaces reify earlier formal and structural orientations. Think about how John Cage used to just stare at the piano in his silence pieces. The instrument was a jumping off point – an interface that had so many routes available. Cage wanted to highlight that meditational aspect of the creative act. The technologies of rhythm science are conduits for the same impulses. The simultaneity of such a variety of source materials and media distinguishes digital composition from its analog predecessors, not to mention the actual physical "dematerialization." In other words, rhythm scientists don't need orchestras; they can simulate them just fine, thanks. It's not so much that the technology changes the compositional process, as extends it into new realms.

Sampling plays with different perceptions of time. Sampling allows people to replay their own memories of the sounds and situations of their lives. Who controls the environment you grew up in? Who controls the situation with which you engage? At the end of the day, it's all about reprocessing the world around you, and this will happen no matter how hard entertainment conglomerates and an older generation of artists tries to control these processes. We're in a delirium of saturation. We're never going to remember anything exactly the way it happened. Memories become ever more fragmented and subjective. Do you want to have a bored delirium or a more exciting one? The archive fever of open system architectures returns us, as I noted earlier, to the era of live jazz and blues sessions, where everyone had access to the same songs, but where they flipped things until they made their own statement. These days everyone and their mother is Dj-ing, so you don't want to just send a basic loop. You've got to give people a sense of total context and environment, which means you've got to be a lot more creative and really open up some new space with your material. It's a lesson learned, because even in the delirium of the archive, part of the creative act is to actually make new stuff. Even a slight shift in frequency pitch or mild sonic flourish changes the original elements you bounce off of. Endlessly reconfigurable and customizable, sampling is dematerialized sculpture.

If I internalize the environment around me, who is going to control how the information eventually resurfaces? It's an uncanny situation; the creative act becomes a dispersion of self. Back in the day, it was called alchemy, but in the hyperfluid environment of information culture, we simply call it the mix. Sampling seen in this light? I like to call it cybernetic jazz.

Making a mix CD is a paradox: it's personal and impersonal, kind of like watching TV using time-shifting software to determine which commercials to cut and which to leave, or like assessing what chess moves to make when you're playing solitaire. Think of downloading your own MP3 file. What sounds would you choose if they were all free? This is all audio alchemy; the order of the tracks is a mode of figuring out which configuration would draw people into my mindset. The order is like "bring people in, open 'em up... show 'em that alchemy flow... and break it down again." That's why I always think of Dj-ing as a crossroads: the virtual style of a culture threaded through fiber optic cables, network systems, the here and now flipped into cipher mode. The code of the new streets, y'all – it's digital. I don't really cook, but I can use a microwave...

IS IT LIVE? OR IS IT A SAMPLE? AFTER ALMOST THREE DECADES OF RHYTHM SCIENCE, THE QUESTION REMAINS JUST AS POWERFUL AS EVER.

UNCANNY/UNWOVEN

A logic of dispersion creates the new gathering spaces, the new cathedrals, the museum and galleries of the phantasmal, the virtual crafts that we use to extend our sense of telepresence. That logic is an old voice emerges singing a new song, a poetry of what cultural theorist Erik Davis calls "the electromagnetic imaginary," and what I call "prosthetic realism." In the movement from Utopia to Heterotopia, the one in the many, the many in the one, we find ourselves caught in a complex web of visual and psychological cues, a form of kinesthethesia that pervades everything we do, an uncanny cipher regulating the traffic of plural meanings that bombard us at every moment.

Art and the imagination – the physical and the mental – join together like the first installment of a loan made from the future. Payment is due. Prosthetic realism – a mirror of the mind as its expression unfolds in time. I break it down with a rhyme: From now to the beginning, let it be like a record spinning/ a poetics of presence/ contents under pressure/got caught in an electromagnetic lecture. As William Carlos Williams observed, "poetry is nothing but a machine made of words." The task of art now is to somehow speak of this plurality of "reals" in a world moving into a polyphrenic cultural space. The Greek agora, the city center, the museum – all these places of social mutuality – find themselves adrift. Art is our guide to the new terrains we have opened within ourselves, in pursuit of techne and logos.

Encoding. What comes to mind when you say the word? Whether it's written or spoken, several meanings emerge and in turn lead you down other paths of meaning. No fixed points come into perspective, no key opens the cryptographic realms of the word to penetration. One simply uses the word to refer to a process.

Encoding. The word evokes systems of thought, procedures of extrapolation, syntax and structure, and most of all a sense of movement and actions taken in a realm of correspondences, of translating one form of code into another. Interpenetration of one form into another mirrors the classic sense of binary movement that writers of semiotic philosophy and literature have been concerned with for several centuries now. Double movement, binary stratification, transience of meaning – all point to a strange game in which absence and presence, form and function, sign and signified, play in an ever-shifting field of meaning, a place where text and textuality switch place with blinding speed. That's what mixing is about: creating seamless interpolations between objects of thought to fabricate a zone of representation in which the interplay of the one and the many, the original and its double all come under question.

Today we live in a society defined – in many senses, and by almost all the connotations associated with the word as well – by the word "current." Alternating or direct, descriptions of transience and modality, in this strange binary world of fiber optics, digital information technologies, and global economics, a logic of alterity is at play. The old hierarchies of linear thought, sublime (and sublimated!) engagements with art, poetry, music, science, and history are no longer needed to do the ideological work now conducted again along the lines of "current." All-inclusive data networks transform individual creation into a kit of interchangeable parts, Lego building blocks of consciousness in a world that moves under the sign of continuous transformation and atomized perspectives. The machinery of culture acts out in the theater of the mind - how we navigate through the abstract systems we use to maintain meaning. As we say in the Dj world, it's all in the mix.

For the most part, creativity rests in how you recontextualize the previous expression of others, a place where there is no such thing as "an immaculate perception." Sampling as the digital equivalent of Feng Shui? Sampling as a kinesthetic theater of memory? Sociosonographic expression – sound writing – mirrors the sense of continuous inscription and re-inscription of text that occurs when the needle, the focal point of sound, electricity, and the refractive characteristics of

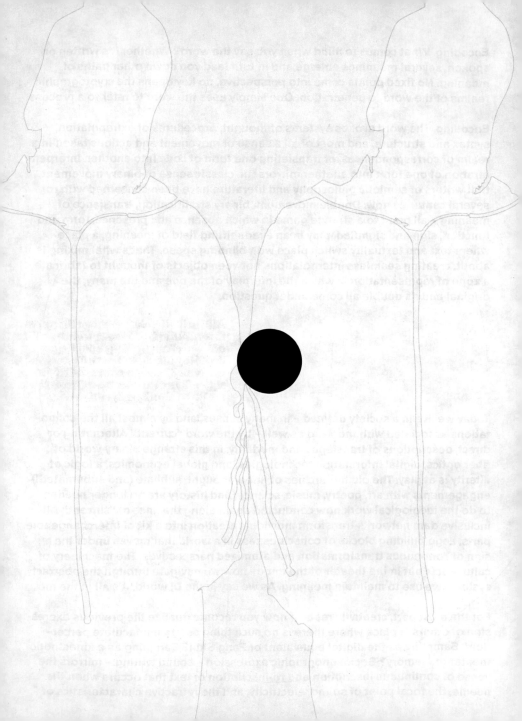

All-inclusive data networks transform individual creation into a kit of interchangeable parts, Lego building blocks of consciousness in a world that moves under the sign of continuous transformation and atomized perspectives.

crystalline structure (the diamond on the tip of the needle), is put into action. The same happens when you press "play" on the cassette deck to make a mix tape, or you ride the fader on the mixing board. Soniture. Ecriture. A phonetics of graphology. Sound and the electric imagination in youth culture as the manifestation of language as total text, or as Toni Morrison puts it in her essay "Playing in the Dark": "The imagination that produces work which bears and invites rereadings, which motions to future readings, as well as contemporary ones, implies a shareable world and an endlesslessly flexible language." Replication as differentiated from mere reproduction. Replication as it stands derived from "reply": the copies transcend the originals, the original is nothing but a collection of previous cultural movements. Flow... The turntable's needle in Dj culture acts as a kind of mediator between self and the fictions of the external world. With the needle the Dj weaves the sounds together. Do you get my drift?

DISTRICTS

I'm a product of Washington, D.C. When I was growing up in the district, the whole world came out of the radio. It was always mixed, and you could check out all sorts of music: rock, dance music, soul, and D.C.'s own unique genre, Go-Go. Go-Go bands like Trouble Funk, Rare Essence, and The Junk Yard Band influenced a lot of hip-hop at that time outside of Washington, but it was electronic in a way that a lot of the Afrika Bambaata/Kraftwerk scene couldn't simulate. In this way, I grew up on "live" electronic music but combined with the dub tradition as well.

I have something between 20,000 and 30,000 records. I inherited my father's collection (he died when I was three years old) and have been building it over the years. I have a wall of records at home that I use; the rest I keep in storage. Sometimes when I look at them or even think about them, I get dizzy with all the voices and potential mixes that I could make. It's infinite and it's heady, and in a sense, all the technology that I use to make my art is corporate. We're so involved with software and hardware that the old notions of left wing–right wing need to be remade, because in an information economy it's all about how information creates identity as a scarce resource. As my mom used to say, "Who speaks through you?"

African-American culture in D.C. was and remains highly segregated. Class and social hierarchies are etched on the whole zone, the city grid and the monuments themselves. Seeing African-American kids drumming on plastic buckets in front of the White House defines the District for me. D.C. was mix culture as dynamic palimpsest – the electromagnetic canvas of a generation raised on and in electricity. That multiplicity really prepared me for the present moment, when even basic software modules for America On-Line come with seven or eight prefabricated personae to use at will to construct on-line identity.

My domestic environment felt more like an academic community, and it was integrated in a complex cultural scene. My father had been dean of the Howard University School of Law. One of my earliest memories is of a piece of newspaper my mom clipped out of the *Washington Post* of him during the Black Panther trials of the early 1970s right before he died. The most controversial phase of his

career was the Angela Davis trial, when she was accused in relation to the "Soledad Brothers" case of kidnapping , murder, and conspiracy. The photo of the bound and gagged Panthers in the courtroom is seared in my memory. Where my Dad was a committed humanist involved with the political and legal turmoil of the late 1960s, my Mom, from that time on up until now, has run a store called "Toast and Strawberries" right off of Dupont Circle. She sells fabrics imported from around the world. The store is a cultural landmark where poetry and culture mingle with fabric – the threads of time hold the tapestry of my youth together. Memories like Sweet Honey in the Rock playing outdoor festivals at Wolftrap, and Donald Bird and The Blackbirds playing at my father's funeral at Howard (Bird had been my father's student) are part of my quilt-work. I pretty much grew up around Connecticut Ave. and Q Street, an area that brought together a lot of the people who populate my childhood – raga kids, punk kids, skateboard kids, you name it – they were hanging out at the Circle.

By the time I was a teenager, the punk rock scene was going on, which engaged on some levels with the conceptual/political art scene. Fugazi was coming out, Minor Threat, Bad Brains. A lot of experimental culture in general, but at the same time, in the black culture scene, I caught a lot of poetry. To me it was much

The turntable's needle in Dj culture acts as a kind of mediator between self and the fictions of the external world. With the needle the Dj weaves the sounds together.

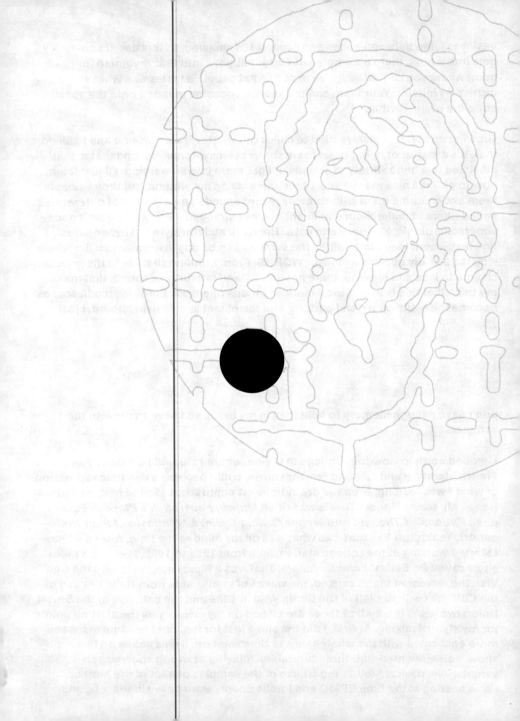

easier to jump between zones and scenes. It's amazing, to this day, if somebody gets into a beat, there's a whole structure that goes into that rhythm to the point where you can actually see exactly what people's tastes are, what weird niche they inhabit. Your taste and preferences become mapped onto the specific structure of the rhythm.

Growing up in D.C., I always tried to check out whatever was around and I still do that. It's a matter of being open to whatever seems interesting, and that makes me listen to a huge variety of sounds. If I get more into something, I'll just learn how to play it. I play many kinds of instruments on my albums, but then I sample them and combine them with scratchy record sounds and a couple of different sound filters to make them sound antique or estranged – you know how it goes – supersonic bionic, as Kool Keith says. The work and the style are hypertextual, one instrument leads to another, the sampler can be any instrument so the whole vibe is basically open to whatever WORKS. From frontier tall tales to the popular cinema to jazz and hip-hop, there are literary and artistic precedents that make me think that this is in fact the American modus operandi. Enfolded mediascapes become the stage on which I perform and the planet is my mixing board. I just

don't have enough memory to hold it all in my brain, so I have to flip into the sampler.

I headed north to Bowdoin College in Maine, where I studied philosophy and French literature and came to feel that music could become a dynamic expression of what I was reading, even the dry, rationalist approaches I found in Kant and Hegel. My senior Honors Thesis was titled *Ludwig Feuerbach's Place in European Rationalist Thought and Wagner's Ring Cycle: A Manifesto of Post-Rational Art*. Yeah, stuff like that was what was on my mind at the time. After a while, I started working at the college station, and, from 1988 to 1992, I hosted a radio show called *Dr. Seuss' Eclectic Jungle*. That was a heady era, what with the Gulf War, the recession that it caused, the waves of immigrants from Haiti, the end of the Cold War with the fall of the Berlin Wall in 1989 and the collapse of the Soviet Union two years later. All of these are etched on my memory as the starting points for my style of mixing. At first, I did the show just for fun, but I became more and more enchanted with the whole thing as time went on. It was chaos on the radio show, noise-oriented with three turntables (playing at wrong speeds) and a sampler-like device. I found the source of the samples of a lot of the hip-hop I was hearing at the time EPMD and Public Enemy were heavy in the mix, and the station had a huge archive so it was easy to find this stuff to play and mix it in. The end result was distorted hip-hop complete with the extra loops I had researched and reassembled.

The environment that I had grown up in, which accepted diversity as a basic way of life, made most of America seem pretty remote. When I graduated, I decided I would be an artist and writer and move to New York City. I wanted to live and breathe in an atmosphere where almost anything seemed possible. At that moment in the early 1990s, Dj-ing seemed the most open thing precisely because it was about THE MIX, and so many other things weren't. I started writing for the *Village Voice*, *Artforum*, and other venues, but when I was writing a lot, dealing with editors was a major drag. The magazines didn't pay that well, and I needed to figure out a scenario to make more cash. I was living in a crazy junkyard on Avenue B and 3rd St. called the Gas Station and, basically, I was broke. My father had left me some money when he died in 1972, but I had blown all of it and that was that. I simply was floating. I had a corner room in the Gas Station where I lived, made the mix tapes, and kept my records. Essentially, the Gas Station was meant to be a studio, and I paid my rent by throwing parties and inviting other

artists to come and participate. I had green dreadlocks and not a care in the world. I thought most of the art in the conventional art world sucked and most of the critics were full of shit. I still think these thoughts, but am mellowed by age. Today, the Gas Station no longer exists. It was paved over and made into a co-op. Bad architecture. Lame building. The memories of those days are gone, and sometimes, I think it's all for the better.

When you Dj, it's just you and the music. That's what art should be about. I created the Dj Spooky persona as a distinct art project and then saw it take on a life of its own in the mixed tape scene of the mid-1990s. Dj Spooky started out as a sticker with a *veve* (a Haitian symbol that is used to summon the spirits in voudoun ceremonies) on the front of the cassettes that I would pass out. The stickers? They said simply, "Who is Dj Spooky?" Stickers are infinite multiples, small spots on the landscape that convey a brief message, a pun, an intent. They were advertisements for myself, missives from a character in a novel that wanted to get in touch with you. Fiction has had stranger characters, but this spooky one was fun because it blurred all of the boundaries. I wrote my text with sound in the events that I played at and passed out commemorative devices to keep the memories fresh in the participants. The sticker and various mix tapes were passed

I DEC
BE AN
WRITI
TO NE
I WAN
AND I
AN AT
WHER
ANYT
POSS

DED I WOULD

ARTIST AND

ER AND MOVE

W YORK CITY.

TED TO LIVE

BREATHE IN

MOSPHERE

E ALMOST

HING SEEMED

IBLE

around, and eventually took on a life of their own. It was before the whole download culture thing, before the webcast, before Napster. Just make a lot of copies of cassettes, pass them around, and see what comes back. They were my own multiple messages in bottles, scraps of magnetic tape thrown out into the ocean of community and alienation in mid-1990s NYC looking for kindred spirits. Dj Spooky washed back onto the shore.

People made copies and passed 'em around. That's the way oral culture works in a world of constantly evolving networks. It's all about relational architecture in the game of the here and

now. Word spreads – you have to think about the way cassettes and now CD-R's circulate in a culture as a kind of underground circuit, a samizdat of sound. There are voices that populate the mix to make it a theater of audio fiction – the mix tape is a work of history on a grand scale, at once sweeping and detailed, closely reasoned and passionately argued. The mix tape paints an unforgettable picture – one alive with conspirators and philosophers, utopians, nihilists, and people who just rhyme about almost anything. It's a parallax view of the modern world where anything goes. It's that simple. Dj Spooky that Subliminal Kid came to define Paul D. Miller as a member of the pop posse, when in fact I'm still an artist and writer at heart. This makes me acutely aware, but from a positive side, of the thrills and perils of multiplex consciousness. Which is not to say that the moment that Dj Spooky emerged from is still with us.

In the early 1990s, that kind of collaged and collated culture stuff was in full swing in the academy at places like Brown University's Semiotics Department and Andrew Ross's American Studies center at NYU. By the close of the decade, Brown's semiotics department was non-existent, and Ross had been put through the ringer in the *Social Text* "science wars" scandal (after the journal's 1996 publication of physicist Alan D. Sokal's tricksterish entrapment, "Transgressing the Boundaries: Towards a Transformative Hermeneutics of Quantum Gravity"). The multicultural vogue – a respect for different approaches to art and culture – was grinding to a halt. The twenty-first century started like a bad cut-up video: too much of everything all the time. By the end of the nineties, the artworld had no need for complex analysis of the multiple paths of info-modernity, and magazines like *21C*, *Art Byte*, or even earlier models like Edit Deak's *Art Rite* (a 1970s maga- zine by and for artists and critics), had all fallen to the wayside. *Jackass* and *Who Wants to Marry A Millionaire* had taken over the discourse machine of the

academy, and even a book with a title like *Philosophy and the Matrix* wouldn't make anyone blink. All of the cultural struggles of the nineties that had motivated me for so long seemed to have been absorbed by the very cultural machinery I had critiqued. As the French say, "*plus ça change…*"

But when I first got to New York, I had started Dj-ing in the same spirit as I'd done the *Eclectic Jungle* show in college. My style was an experiment with rhythm and clues, rhythm and cues: Drop the needle on the record and see what happens when this sound is applied to this context, or when that sound crashes into that recording. The first impulses I had about Dj culture were taken from that basic idea – play and irreverence toward the found objects that we use as consumers and a sense that something new was right in front of our oh-so-jaded eyes. I wanted to breathe a little life into the passive relationship we have with the objects around us and to bring a sense of permanent uncertainty about the role of art in our lives. For me, as an artist, writer, and musician, it seemed that turnta- bles were somehow imbued with the art of being memory permutation machines. They changed how I remembered sounds and always made me think of a different experience with each listening.

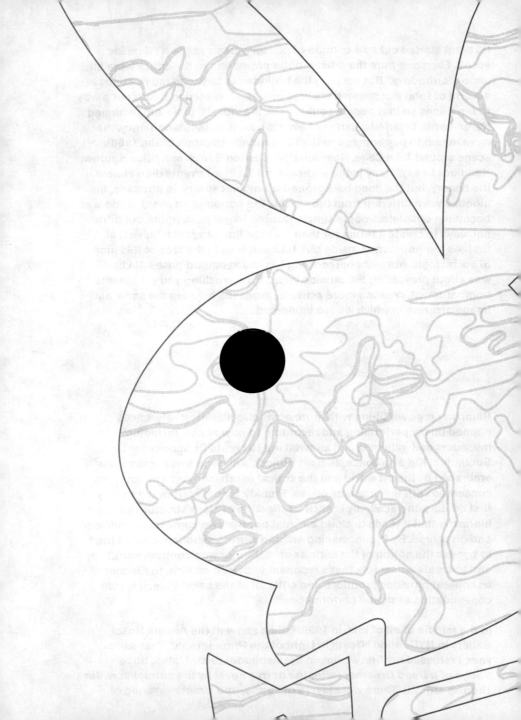

ILLbient started out as a critique of conservatisms in the NYC music scene. Everyone from the artists to the promoters to the critics were all about "orthodoxy." But keeping the boundaries between music styles in a world of total flux seemed crazy to me, and I wanted to figure out a way to flip things so that people could check the vibe. With a woman named Karen Levitt, I started a series of events based on indeterminancy, that were meant to pay homage to the Happenings tradition of the 1960s scene around John Cage, Nam Jun Paik, Joseph Beuys, and Allan Kaprow. Needless to say, many in the audience for ILLbient events didn't know the history, but the deep background wasn't necessary. In any case, the nineties were different from the sixties, the notion of an avant garde was becoming obsolete. People simply wanted to get paid, figure out different ways to create a forum for their zone to flow, and then leave it at that. As hip-hop turned inside out, ILLbient flew in the face of this kind of social logic, but without resorting to tired vanguard poses. ILLbient was about preventing the outside world from crushing you with media bombardment, creating more active approaches to using the sonic and image archives in which we are immersed.

Remixing my own Dj-ing with more aesthetic-historical references opened up my performing and recording to new zones, including museums and galleries, and allowed me to create Dj Spooky that Subliminal Kid as a conceptual art project. Although this persona was embraced by the art world and the critical establishment, I'm not really concerned with the academy per se. Frankly, by the start of the twenty-first century, the academy is such a reflection of class structure and hierarchy that it tends to cloud any real progressive contexts of criticism and discourse. By Dj-ing, making art, and writing simultaneously, I tried to bypass the notion of the critic as an authority who controls narrative, and to create a new role that's resonant with web culture: to function as content provider, producer, and critic all at the same time. It is role consolidation as digital performance.

In the middle of all of this, in 1996, I did a show at the Annina Nosei Gallery in NYC called "Death in Light of the Phonograph." That same year, I released my first album on the Asphodel record label, titled *Songs of a Dead Dreamer* (after the horror novel by the surrealist writer Thomas Ligotti). There were layers of sound, and a meta-layering of commentary and even inside jokes in the sounds I was using. Debussy, North African Moroccan music, funk, electronic feedback, music from the sound-track to the British SF television show, *Doctor Who*. All of that material got mixed, spliced, and diced – collaged. Nothing was meant to stand alone. The mix was meant to be a piece of audio sculpture, and the gallery show was meant to highlight the linkages between physical sculpture and sound. At the time, I was obsessed with death, with mortality, with sound and memory carrying shards of both. I wanted to figure out a way to create a simulation of myself in sound, a digital exorcism of the toxic things our culture does to us as it creates us. In essence, the show was way over-conceptualized. The art work didn't sell. But the *Songs of a Dead Dreamer* CD did.

Then, in 1998, I got picked up by Geffen Records, for my major label debut. *Riddim Warfare* was a critique of the hypocrisy and sheer conservatism that drives the culture scenes – hip-hop, dancehall reggae, academia, you name it. People are so programmed to accept a media construct that if something isn't affirmed by their peers and/or mass culture, then it might as well not exist. *Riddim Warfare* is Cliff Notes for the sonically perplexed. Riddim is open. Riddim is a vehicle anyone

can use. Riddim is a blank slate that accepts all images, all performers. It's instrumental – the reason goes with the rhyme. Again, the loop folds back. Blip, bleep: reset: rewind. *Riddim Warfare* was a bridge between the way we think and the way we live. The boundaries are all in place, it's just about bypassing the strictures, and seeing what new modes develop. The Japanese artist Mariko Mori contributed a buddhist mantra – *mono ni kami* – that held the album together. A rhyme from Pharaoh Monk about reconstruction was interpreted in light of W.E.B. Du Bois. Do these claims of multiplicity stand alone? No. The fight is against one-track minds. Hearing a mono signal in this era is about the same as wearing a scarlet letter in another. Both are emblems of obsolescence, of socially enforced mores that damage everyone who agrees to them. With *Riddim Warfare*, I strove to create pan-humanist metaphors. Again, these are always metaphors, and the only thing that I really think made it all come together wasn't the album – it was the performances. Then Geffen was acquired by Universal, they switched the deal, fired the people I'd been working with, and I haven't been with a major label since. In fact, I've determined that I don't need to be. In this day and age, given shareware culture and its impact on those so-called majors, artists can and should build their own platforms and can have as big an impact – if they pay attention to the game.

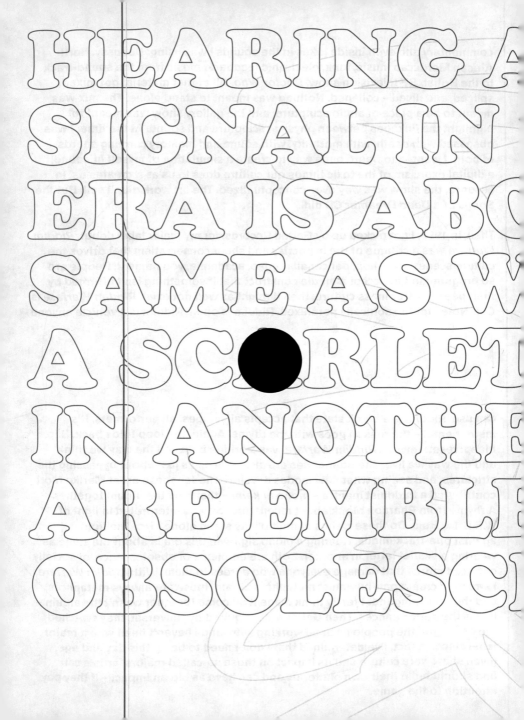

HEARING A
SIGNAL IN
ERA IS AB
SAME AS W
A SC●RLET
IN ANOTHE
ARE EMBL
OBSOLESC

MONO

THIS

UT THE

EARING

LETTER

R. BOTH

MS OF

ENCE

In 1999, I did a CD with the British sound artist Scanner, *The Quick and the Dead*. This CD involved me culling through fragments of my recordings of environments and Scanner going through his recordings of all of the different frequencies that make up the urban landscape. Call it a "critique of the invisible" if you will, but the point was that records operate on the level of frequencies as well – transmission mode "open" - and the sense was of dematerialized sculpture with the city as source material. Hip-hop made from the "streets" of the frequencies that are coming to mean more than the physical world they inhabit and describe. Culture is "a system being consumed by our communications technologies," as German media philosopher Friedrich Kittler puts it. On the track, "Synchronism 2," Marshall McLuhan's voice informs us that "electric circuitry... the flowing" is taking us on an "inner

trip... which involve us in depth in things that had formerly been merely superficial, visual, external and detached from our own beings." Arguably, the opposite has been true of our relationship to technology in the late stages of capital accumulation: the specialization, fragmentation, and routineization of work, space and life. In an era of shortened attention spans, we thought it was important to make sure that *The Quick and The Dead* was all about flow.

For the next several years I spent much of my time Dj-ing on an increasingly international circuit: Australia, Brazil, Japan, India, Russia. All these distant lands became my home away from home in music. I finished several other albums – all increasingly taking on the roles of chapter titles in a novel made of music, my version of Jorge Luis Borges's "The Garden of Forking Paths" (Dj Spooky remix).

In 2002, I made a strategic side-step into jazz with *Optometry* and *Dubtometry*. *Optometry* plays with the historical mystique of the jazzman, remixed through digital media. I asked free jazz musicians like Matthew Shipp, William Parker, and Guillermo Brown, the poet Carl Hancock Rux, and legendary horn player Joe Mcphee, along with a host of host of others, to contribute sound elements to the mix. I took their elements – voices, bass solos, drum solos, horn riffs – and created a tapestry. The vibe on this is "sampling as a new form of jazz." I was thinking back on Duke Ellington's "Afro-Eurasian Eclipse," Dizzy Gillespie's "Anthropology," Miles Davis's "On the Corner," John Coltrane and Don Cherry's "The Avant Garde," anything by Nina Simone, the music of the Jamaican and Caribbean diaspora, Ralph Ellison's sound lectures, Maya Deren's Haitian ballet studies, even Yoko Ono's primal scream poems, and Karlheinz Stockhausen and Nam June Paik's satellite compositions. *Optometry* is about all of that as an echo of the hero-and-now. *Optometry* is synaesthetic, skewing the sciences of perception: seeing sound, hearing vision.

Dubtometry took the core elements of the finished *Optometry* project and sent them to dub masters Mad Professor and Lee "Scratch" Perry. From *Optometry*

to *Dubtometry*, we shift into the griot's realm of wordplay. *Dubtometry* treats jazz as a found object, and all the elements of the "original" *Optometry* album are there to be played with. In Jamaica, the dub masters call it "versioning." In modernism, think of Robert Rauschenberg buying a drawing in 1953 from Willem de Kooning, only to erase it, an act that Jasper Johns called "additive subtraction." In *Dubtometry*, the soundscape is a palimpsest that encourages play. This project is less about Harold Bloom's anxiety of influence than the development of a community of exchange. That sense of a community is what pan-humanism is about, moving beyond the parochial identity politics of the 1990s. The mix in *Dubtometry* moves beyond the codifications of rhythm that conventional Dj culture forces people to adhere to. No, don't play a set that moves at 95 beats per minute for an hour. No, don't play a set that chugs along at 120 beats per minute forever. With *Optometry* and *Dubtometry*, I wanted to create exchange as dialog, to have the remix become a vector of cultural infection. Dub speaks from erasure, the voice fragmented and left to drift on the shards of itself that are left when its body is taken away. Dub speaks of invocations and quotations. Jazz updates the formula. Constantly.

**have the remix become a
vector of cultural infection.**

DJ-ING IS WRITING/WRITING IS DJ-ING

Writing becomes your own temple and you just move in and make sure everything flows and the right divinities are in effect.

As a Dj, an artist, and a writer, I do what I enjoy. If I didn't like it, I wouldn't do it. If you follow through with whatever you're into, you can do it. It doesn't matter if it's not consistent, there's a market or niche for every possible endeavor under the sun.

Writing may be a little retro, but that's cool, too. That's why people still wear bell-bottom jeans. You can always squeeze some-thing out of the past and make it become new. Writing keeps me sane. I love my work as a Dj and the rush from the crowd. I enjoy the challenges of multimedia and the technological jolt you get in the studio – even the

direct connections you make speaking before an audiences. But there's something about the labor or writing and the sense of being part of the continuum
of writing that goes back thousands of years. It is an ancient form, and in some
ways it doesn't quite fit what's happening. The challenge then is to describe or
characterize what it feels like to be alive now in the midst of it, but using this
other mode of communication. I know people who are totally electronic and it's
fascinating to see them, but in some ways their consciousness works differently
than mine. I'm still part of Gutenberg's Galaxy. There's a reflexivity that comes
with having to compose and letting language come through you. It's a different
speed, there's a slowness there. And I'm attracted to writing's infectiousness, the
way you pick up language from other writers and remake it as your own.

This stance is not contradictory: Dj-ing is writing, writing is Dj-ing. Writing is
music, I cannot explain this any other way. Take Nietzsche, for instance, whose
brilliant texts are almost musical. Obviously, you feel the rhythm inside a great
poet's stanzas, but it's there within the great philosophers' paragraphs as well.
So many media and cultural techniques of interpretation coexist – reading,
watching, listening, surfing, dancing – that this textual/sonic synasthesia

demands a great deal from us. Yet in pop culture, that deadly inertia I mentioned
earlier can put a stop to the idealism of coexistence. People can become so
unreflective in their usual media-habits that any kind of systemic renewal takes
a long time to succeed.

Saying that people are literate means that they have read widely enough to refer-
ence texts, to put them in a conceptual framework. They are capable of creating
an overview. This kind of literacy exists in the musical arena, too. The more you
have heard, the easier it is to find links and to recognize quotations. To specialize
in either music or literature you need months, years of reading or listening to
music. But the difference is that people have a more emotional approach toward
music. If you don't like a book, you put it aside after the first few pages. As for the
philosophical or theoretical component in my music, I do know that average kids
from the street are probably not aware of the connections between Derrida's
deconstructions and turntablism's mixes, but it's there if they ever come looking,
and my own writings are a place to start.

Writing becomes your own temple and you just move in and make sure everything
flows and the right divinities are in effect. It's a puzzle you set for yourself. Being

Writing becomes your own temple and you just move in and make sure everything flows and the right divinities are in effect.

MULTIPLEX CONSCIOUSNESS

the MULTIPLEX CONSCIOUSNESS full immersed in and defined by the data surrounds it, we are entering an era o multiplex consciousness.

at a crossroads and questioning how far to push writing, or music, or art, uncertain which direction to move, is actually a good thing, because it forces me to go back to the basic issues. Why do I want to write, why do I want to make a track, why do I want to do this installation? They're all hobbies, which keeps the fun. If I were a dead serious artist guy, who wanted to just strictly be in all the right collections, and network the gallery scene, that's easily done. Same with the Dj

circuit. But by being a hobbyist, a kind of *flaneur* or somebody who jumps around, it keeps things fresh and new. I can only imagine what kind of mentality most people must have doing one thing all their lives. Because I grew up with books, I've always wanted to write them, to add my own contribution to the mind's bookshelf.

At the end of the day, I write because I want to communicate with fellow human beings and forestall subjective implosion.

Dj culture is more than just technologically multiplex. There's the whole issue of personal identity: African-American, Irish-American, Jewish-American, Arab-American, Hispanic-American, Asian-American. Scratch the surface-level homogeneity and America's deep ethnic schizophrenia is going surface. No one can escape an identity clash if they bounce of off the "received culture" of commercialized information, not even WASPs. Identity is about creating an environment where you can make the world act as your own reflection.

One hundred years ago, in his searing work, *The Souls of Black Folk*, W.E.B. Du Bois contributed the concept of "double consciousness" to the American dialogue. "Born with a veil, and gifted with a second sight in this American world," Du Bois wrote of the African American condition, we are faced with "a world which yields... no true self consciousness, but only lets [us] see [ourselves] through the revelation of the other world. It is a peculiar sensation, this double consciousness, this sense of always looking at oneself through the eyes of others...one ever feels his two-ness – an American, a Negro; two souls, two thoughts, two unreconciled strivings, two warring ideals in one dark body, whose dogged strength alone keeps it from being torn asunder."

Jazz great Charles Mingus moved beyond Du Bois's dualities at the beginning of his autobiography, *Beneath the Underdog*, to a form of triple consciousness: "In other words, I am three. One man stands forever in the middle, unconcerned, unmoved, watching, waiting to be allowed to express what he sees to the other two." Mingus shows us a third path and, in a sense, continues the dialogue around how much people need "franchise identity" to modulate their perceptions of themselves. Where Du Bois saw duality and Mingus imagined a trinity, I would say that the twenty-first-century self is so fully immersed in and defined by the data that surrounds it, we are entering an era of multiplex consciousness.

To claim multiplex consciousness is not to deny the racial oppression that prompted Du Bois's initial interest in duality. African-American culture went through a cycle of extreme flux during the slave period to create a milieu where everything, down even to the words spoken, were the equivalent of a "found object." Slavery followed by segregation created so strong a pattern of overlapping dualities that it prefigured aspects of on-line culture. What Paul Gilroy called the "Black Atlantic" is just a small part of the ocean of rhythm science. All the issues involved with aliases, multiple narrative threading, social engineering environments, and identity as a social cipher are tropes brought to the forefront

the twenty-first-century self is so fully immersed in and defined by the data that surrounds it, we are entering an era of multiplex consciousness.

of immigrant culture in America. When the slave experience of cultural erasure encountered the immigrant phenomenon of identity
reconstruction in the city, the culture as a whole moved away from
the melting pot model to becomes a frequency centrifuge: cultures
in conflict, messages etched and pasted on every street corner,
images raining down, thoughts like rain, the city fragments and coa-
lesces. Freud used to call the situation "unheimlich" or "uncanny"
but the sense of alienation and familiarity is reminiscent of the
Situationist critique of the urban landscape. They simply called it
"psychogeographic" – the layers of the city unfold in the mind of the
person who moves through the landscape. What could be a better
parallel to "systems culture" where everyone can contribute to
rhythm science; whether it's Linux, or hip-hop, or mix-tape culture.

Afro-Diasporic culture was the first Generation X. The current multi-
valent entity we call the United States is enthralled with the unconscious implications of Africa in the New World. One of the most
progressive developments over the last decade was the explosion

in youth culture's engagement with electronic media through hip-
hop. The multiplex consciousness of rhythm science adds several
layers of complexity: the "current" – all puns intended, alternating
and direct – has been deleted. Any sound can be you. It's an emotion
of abstraction and attention deficit disorder. There's so much information about who you should be or what you should be that you're
not left with the option of trying to create a mix of your very self.
Mix culture, with its emphasis on exchange and nomadism, serves
as a precedent for the hypertextual conceits that later arrived from
the realms of the academy. The mix absorbs almost anything it can
engage – and much that it can't. In the context of jazz and blues,
emotion and catharsis become cyberneticly coded structure. Identi-
fication and cathexis: examine the etymology of the word "phonograph" for a similar logic. Phono/graph means sound/writing and
in an era of rhythm science both serve as recursive aspects of information collage where everything from personal identity to the codes
used to create art or music are available for the mix. It's that simple
and it's that complex.

Identity, both nodal and distributed, is key. Sampling, Dj culture, and the hip-hop zone are founded on ancestor worship and the best rhythm scientists are constantly expanding the pantheon. The music itself is far more dynamic than many of the people who make it. Hell, Walt Whitman lived in Brooklyn, the same borough as Biggie Smalls. "So what if I contradict my self - I am large, I contain multitudes," is a famous line, but it could just as easily have been Biggie's as Whitman's. There has always been an American hybrid multicultural scene, and the music was always a reflection of that. The computer's ubiquity means that that hybridity is now migrating over to the visual and artistic realms. In that sense, music was out in front and out of sync with the rest of the sound and image tracks of the American dream. It's still ahead of the ballgame though, 'cause people simply do not know how to check out different zones and "parlay," as Grand Puba, the lead rapper for Brand Nubian, used to say. Dj culture tells us that the music speaks louder than any individual voice.

Rhythm science builds on the early successes of file-sharing to create a milieu where people can exchange culture and information at will and create new forms, new styles, new ways of thinking. The Dj spreads a memetic contagion, a thought

storm brought about by annoyance and frustration with almost all the conventional forms of race, culture, and class hierarchies. Hip-hop is a vehicle for that, and so are almost all forms of electronic music. At their best, these genres are about the morphology of structure – how forms and feelings transmute from one medium to another. Culture in this milieu affects a dialectical triangulation. Language become its own form of digital code... check the theater of the rhyme as it unfolds in time.

Hip-hop is always innovative and it can absorb almost anything. This is not to deny that there are boundaries about how new sounds can be spread. When people are faced with conditions where "conservatives" control the zone, they have to innovate to get their message out, but innovation leads to constant elevation. It's less Social Darwinism than a cooperative model of how information spreads in the hothouse environment of net-culture where "newness" is celebrated with how many people check in on the information. And if the spread of virus, worms, and internet urban legends are any indication, this kind of hacked "social engineering" can happen with an ease far and above almost any word-of-mouth situation in human history. I'm just happy to be around to see if it can change even more.

SAMPLING, DJ CULTURE, AND THE HIP-HOP ZONE ARE FOUNDED ON ANCESTOR WORSHIP AND THE BEST RHYTHM SCIENTISTS ARE CONSTANTLY EXPANDING THE PANTHEON.

PHONOGRAPHY

Rhythm science has a history to go along with its future. Back in 1875, ten years after the Civil War demolished half of the United States, the poet Ralph Waldo Emerson wrote an essay that prefigured much of the discourse around "originality" in twenty-first-century culture. In "Quotation and Originality," Emerson tried to come to grips with a cultural inertia that he saw in the literature of his day. The central premise of his essay was that people's minds were so burdened with the weight of previous creative work that they were too often forced to simply take elements from the past and reconfigure them to their own, contemporary. "Our debt to tradition through reading and conversation is so massive, our protest so rare and insignificant – and this common-ly on the ground of other reading or hearing – that in large sense, one would say there is no pure original-ity. All minds quote. Old and new make the warp and

woof of every moment. There is no thread that is not a twist of these two strands." But Emerson took the occasion of this essay to look beneath the surface that this cultural saturation fostered. He wrote redemptively, "By necessity, by proclivity, and by delight, we all quote." And, he goes on to note something that conservative critics of hip-hop will never understand: "It is as difficult to appropriate the thoughts of others as it is to invent."

Two years later, in 1877, Thomas Edison did invent something new, the phonograph, which added a wrinkle to the mix. The phonograph, or "talking machine," or even "the memory machine," recorded the human voice onto a tinfoil roll. The first record-ing was of Edison reciting "Mary Had a Little Lamb," and was the embodiment of Edison's search for a simpler, more easily controlled method of creating music. Edison was under the influence of Herman von Helmholtz, one of the first scientists to critique sound from the viewpoint of physics, who advanced a notion of a "science of the beautiful" based on tone structure and its replication in music. Von Helmholtz's theories had a massive influence on Edison, who felt that his inventions were mechanical ways to, in his words, "establish music on a scientific basis." "You know music in one way," Edison would say to his friends with formal training, "and I in another - I know nothing about musical notation and have never tried to learn. I am glad that I don't know. I try to form my own opinions."

The phonograph becomes the bedrock of a rhythm science that links Edison to Emerson. This connection is more than just the serendipity of chronological and geographical juxtaposition. Edison viewed Emerson as his life-long mentor. In *Edison: Inventing the Century*, biographer Neil Baldwin wrote about this relationship as being a kind of rough and tumble trade-off between the pragmatic inventor and the lofty poet. For Baldwin, Edison's initial discoveries and deployments of his mechanical and electric devices led him in time to invent things that were a way of trying to deal with America's expansionist urges. Edison viewed his invention of the phonograph as a method of having access to the past – some-

today, the voice may not be you

thing that would make it more than just a phantasm of collective memory. Edison liked to compare himself to the turntables he invented. "I am," he would say while boasting about his technical efficiency, "like a phonograph." But the prosthetic relationship between voice, memory, and the devices we use to recall them to our "pre-sent" selves is not a new issue. As Emerson noted in "Quotation and Originality," the dialectic between memory and inertia has haunted the notion of human identity for millennia. In this way, the inventor's "phonograph," the talking machine that gives us a "phonetics of graphology," is as old as the human voice and materializes the poet's analysis of "the warp and woof of every moment."

Recording the voice proposes an ontological risk. The recorded utterance is the stolen sound that returns to the self as the schizophonic, hallucinatory, presence of another. But today, the voice you speak with may not be your own. The mechanization of war, the electro-colonization of information, the hypercommidification of culture, the exponential growth of mass media – all of these point to a machinic/semiotic hierarchy of representation that models human thought as a distributed network. Rhythm science is performed in a place where consciousness itself becomes an object of "material memory." The spread of global networks of all sort (information distribution systems, mail systems, direct satellite

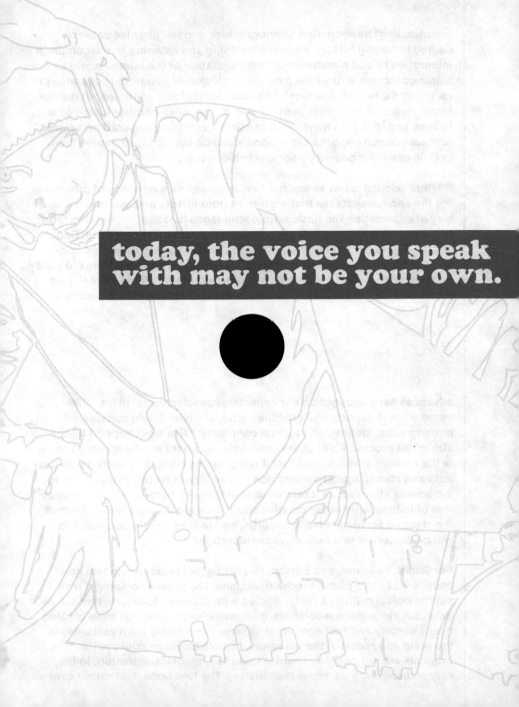

**today, the voice you speak
with may not be your own.**

broadcasting) have created phonographies and telephonies unprece-
dented in human history. We are witnessing and listening to the complete
integration of and simultaneous representation of the human world as a
single conscious entity based on the implosion of geographic distance or
cartographic failure. The mesh of sound, symbol and sentiment that electronic music represents is another way of speaking, another fusion of arte,
techne, and logos – a melding of the Greek words for art, craft and word.
Rhythm science imposes order upon skill and the ability to deploy them
both in electro-modernity's sociographic space.

Rhythm science is not so much a new language as a new way of pronouncing the ancient syntaxes that we inherit from history and evolution, a new
way of enunciating the basic primal languages that slip through the fabric
of rational thought and infect our psyche at another, deeper level. Could
this be the way of healing? Taking elements of our own alienated consciousness and recombining them to create new languages from old (and
in doing so to reflect the chaotic turbulent reality we all call home), just
might be a way of seeking to reconcile the damage rapid technological

advances have wrought on our collective consciousness. In his 1966
essay, "The Prospects of Recording," pianist Glenn Gould considered
phonography, identity, and textual continuity: "The most hopeful thing
about this process – about the inevitable disregard for the identity factor
in the creative situation – is that it will permit a climate in which biological
data and chronological assumption can no longer be the cornerstone for
judgments about art as it relates to environment. In fact, this whole situation of individuality in the creative situation – the process through which
the creative act results from, absorbs, and re-forms individual opinion –
will be subjected to a radical reconsideration."

For Gould, Emerson, and Edison, recreating and reproducing text and
sounds was not a purely mechanical issue. The process created it own
psychological culture, a realm riddled with paradox. Today, rhythm scientists operate under a recombinant aesthetic with roots that were planted
over a century and half ago. What differentiates today from yesterday is
the scale and scope of the paradigm. In 1875 Emerson could write: "The
originals are not original. There is imitation, model, suggestion, to the
very archangels, if we knew their history. The first book, tyrannizes over

the second." Today we have an entire youth culture based on the premise of replication, which itself derives from the word "reply." Ours is a milieu in which much of what is heard, seen, and thought, is basically a refraction of the electronicized world that we have built around ourselves.

Emerson's critique of how people absorb text closely parallels one of the first recorded copyright disputes in Western history. In sixth-century Ireland, Christianity was a fairly recent import, and almost all of the sacred manuscripts were copies. So, when St. Columba borrowed a manuscript of the Latin Psalter from Finnian of Druim Finn, it was not an unusual step for Columba to make a copy. Finnian, the original "owner," protested, demanding both his lent manuscript and the new copy back. The king at that time ruled for Finnian, with the immortal phrase, "As the calf belongs to the cow, so the copy belongs to its book." The two disputing parties went to war, with St. Columba, the "copyright violator," winning on the field and holding on to his copy of the Gospels. The violence inherent in the battle to control and distribute culture continues from Columba's time through Guttenberg, Emerson, Edison, and Gould, and holds true today, when record companies sue college students who download music over the net.

In another light, Emerson and St. Columba parallel the thoughts and observations of one of the original "structuralist" thinkers, the eighteenth-century Italian author Giambattista Vico, who refined his concept of "poetic wisdom" through the writing his major work, *The New Science*. Intellectual historian Donald Philip Verene refers to *The New Science* as a "a theater of memory," in which sound works as a kind of zone of aberration, a place where many of the cultural motifs that "the ancients" used were able to be passed down through time in a process of continuous cultural combat between the elements of the new and old. In the epochal *New Science*, Vico explores "the physics of man," a place where human value structures continuously evolve and change in response to the underlying myths that hold together the fabric of their cultures: "Philosophers and philologists should be concerned in the first place with poetic metaphysics; that is, the science that looks for proof not in the external world, but in the very modifications of the mind that meditates on it. Since the world of nations is made by men, it is inside their minds that its principles should be sought." Vico always refers to myths as the underlying forces driving the unconscious impulses of culture. Earlier in his explorations of cultural transformation and his "physics of man" he posits "contests of song" as a way of transferring the values of society from generation to generation. "The civil institutions in use under such kingdoms," he

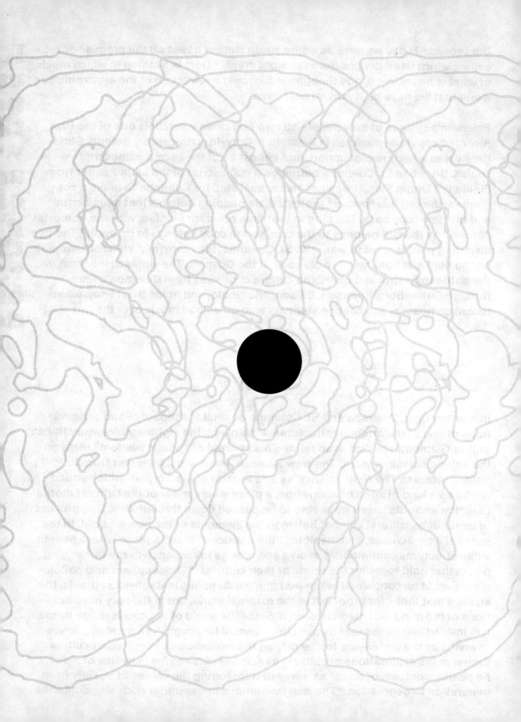

Rhythm science is not so much a new language as a new way of pronouncing the ancient syntaxes that we inherit from history and evolution, a new way of enunciating the basic primal languages that slip through the fabric of rational thought and infect our psyche at another, deeper level.

writes of "the ancients," are in a way always mediated by the way they engage the culture that generated their "auspices." He continues, the civil institutions "are narrated for us by poetic history in the numerous fables that deal with contests of song... and consequently refer to the heroic contests over the auspices... Thus the satyr Marsyas...when overcome by Apollo in a contest of song, is flayed alive by the god... the sirens, who lull sailors to sleep with their song and then cut their throats; the Sphinx, who puts riddles to travelers and slays them on their failure to find a solution... all these portray the politics of the heroic cities. The sailors, travelers, and wanderers of these fables are the aliens."

Emerson, like Vico before him, develops his argument for a kind of respectful synthesis at the core of how culture evolves and changes. Midway through "Quotation and Originality," we find him quoting Goethe, who as far as we know, was probably quoting someone else: "Our country, our customs, laws, our ambitions, and our notions of fit and fair – all these we never

made, we found them ready made; we but quote them." Goethe frankly admitted, "What would remain to me if this art of appropriation were derogatory to genius? Every one of my writings has been furnished to me by a thousand different persons, a thousand things: wise and foolish have brought me, without suspecting it, the offering of their thoughts, faculties and experience. My work is an aggregation of beings taken from the whole of nature. It bears the name of Goethe."

Today's notion of creativity and originality are configured by velocity: it is a blur, a constellation of styles, a knowledge and pleasure in the play of surfaces, a rejection of history as objective force in favor of subjective interpretations of its residue, a relish for copies and repetition, and so on. We inhabit a cultural zone informed by what Giles Deleuze liked to call a "logic of the particular," a place where the subjective, multiple, interpretations of information lead us to take the real as a kind of consensual, manufactured situation. Where does this ebb and flow that both Emerson and Columba seem to be arguing for, fit in? There

: so
as a
:ng
:hat
ry
way
sic
: slip

infect
:,

seems to be some sort of confusion as to whether previous migrations of meaning ever actually reached the dense locale of late twentieth-century youth culture. For that is, after all, a place where many of the issues that drive the discourses of both cultural criticism and philosophy tend to be generated and played out. We live in a time where the human body is circumscribed by a dense locale of technological sophistry: a place where the line dividing the organic and inorganic elements that form the core essence of human life is blurring. Unravel the distortions of the present day. Sampling is like sending a fax to yourself from the sonic debris of a possible future; the cultural permutations of tomorrow, heard today, beyond the corporeal limits of the imagination.

RHYTHMIC CINEMA

With rhythm science, what the Surrealists called "automatic writing" – transforming subconscious thoughts into formalized artistic acts – gets flipped, becomes a gangsta dreamtime remix. Rhythm science models itself on open-source Linux-coded operating systems, becomes a mode of psychogeographic shareware for the open market in a world where identity is for sale to the highest bidder. Screen time. Prime Time: Life as a boundless-level video game with an infinite array of characters to pick from. Poker-faced, the dealer tells you, "Pick a card, any card." It's a game that asks, "Who speaks through you?" There are a lot of echoes in the operating system, but that's the point. The game goes on. The moment of revelation is encoded in the action. You become the star of the scene, your name etched in bullets ripping through the crowd. Neon lit social

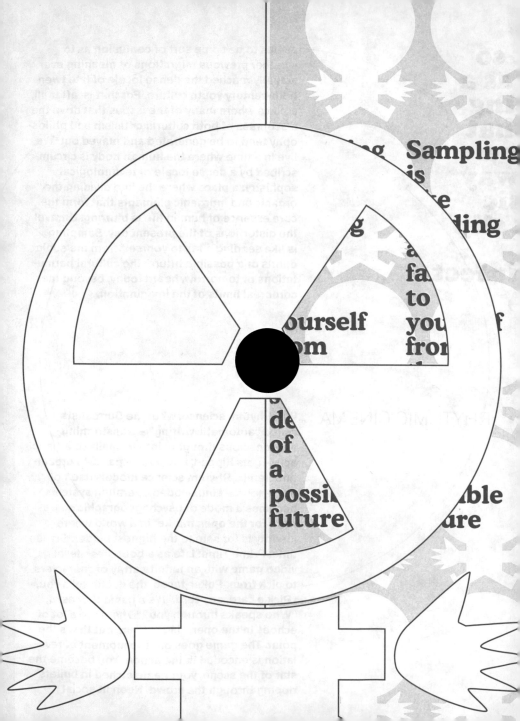

Sampling is like sending a fax to yourself from the sonic debris of a possible future

Sampling is like sending a fax to yourself from the sonic debris of a possible future

Sampling is like sending a fax to yourself from the sonic debris of a possible future

Sampling is like sending a fax to yourself from the sonic debris of a possible future

Darwinism for the technicolor age. Set your browser to drift mode and simply float: The sequence really doesn't care what you do as long as you are watching. "Now" becomes a method for exploring the coded landscapes of contemporary post-industrial reality, a hypgnagogic flux, a Situationist reverie, a psychogeography – a dérive without beginning or end. Ask any high school student in the United states and they can tell you the same thing, but with a different set of references.

Most people trace the idea of time without variation to Newton's 1687 *Principia*. With the term "absolute time," he created a sense that the world moved in a way that only allowed for one progression, one sequence of actions. Newton's synchronized time ordered the Industrial Revolution and gave us a culture of production based on highly stratified temporal regulation. Two hundred fifty years later, Andre Bréton and the Surrealists strove to escape from Newton's straightjacket into moments of "total freedom." They found that freedom in the abandonment of the roles that they, like everyone else around them, were forced to play. Flip the script, timestretch the code. That most twenty-first-century of catchphrases, "Money is time, but time is not money," is yet another attitude we inherit form the past century: from the "clockwork economy" of Frederick Winslow Taylor's

Principles of Scientific Management in 1911 on up to the hypercondensed aesthetics of commercials and videos on MTV.

What happens when you look at the time part of the phrase, "money is time?" A paradox in math and physics translates into the social realm of human relations. What would happen if the uncanny system of correspondences that make up the components of reality stopped? What would we do if that place where all the stories come from suddenly vanished like a mirage in the desert of our collective dreams? As the amount of information out there explodes exponentially and threatens to become almost the only way people relate to one another, it's a question that seems to beg a response: What would happen if it just vanished and the lights went out?

Sometimes the best way to get an idea across is to simply tell it as a story. It's been a while since the autumn day in 1896 when Georges Méliès was filming a late afternoon Paris crowd caught in the ebb and flow of the city's traffic. One of those random occurrences that always seem to be at the core of history then took place. Méliès was in the process of filming an omnibus as it came out of a tunnel, and his camera jammed. He tried for several moments to get it going again, but with no luck. After a couple of minutes he got it working again, and the camera's lens caught a hearse going by. It was an accident that went unnoticed until he got home. When the film was developed and projected it seemed as if the bus morphed into a funeral hearse and back to its original form again. In the space of what used to be called *actualités* – real contexts reconfigured into stories that the audiences could relate to – a simple opening and closing of a lens had placed the viewer in several places and times simultaneously. In the space of one random error, Méliès created what we know of today as the "cut" – words, images, sounds flowing out the lens projection would deliver, like James Joyce used to say "sounds like a river." Flow, rupture, and fragmentation – all seamlessly bound to the viewer's perspectival architecture of film and sound, all utterly malleable – in the blink of an eye space and

time as the pre-industrial culture had known it came to an end.

Whenever you look at an image or listen to a sound, there's a ruthless logic of selection that you have to go through to simply to create a sense of order. The end product on this palimpsest of perception is a composite of all the thoughts and actions you sift through over the last several micro-seconds – a soundbite reflection of a process that updates Frankenstein's monster, but this time the imaginary creature is made of the interplay fragments of time, code, and (all puns intended) memory and flesh. The eyes stream data to the brain through something like two million fiber bundles of nerves. Consider the exponential aspects of perception when you multiply this kind of density by the fact that not only does the brain do this all the time, but the millions of bits of information streaming through your mind at any

UTHLE
OGIC O
ELECTI

RUTHLESS LOGIC OF SELECTION

moment have to be coordinated and like the slightest rerouting is, like the hearse and omnibus of Méliès film accident, any shift in the traffic of information can create not only new thoughts, but new ways of thinking. Literally. Nonfiction, check the meta-contradiction... back in the early portion of the twentieth century this kind of emotive fragmentation implied a crisis of representation, and it was filmmakers, not Djs, who were on the cutting edge of how to create a kind of subjective intercutting of narratives and times. D. W. Griffith was known as "the man who invented Hollywood," and the words he used to describe his style of composition –"intra-frame narrative," the "cut-in," the "cross-cut" – staked out a space in America's linguistic terrain. While *Birth of a Nation*, Griffith's most famous work, was indeed used as a recruitment film for the Ku Klux Klan at least up until the mid-1960s, this film's impact on our culture can't be understated. When President Woodrow Wilson saw it for the first time, he was prompted to claim it was "like writing history with lightning." I wonder what President Wilson would have said of Grand Master Flash's 1981 classic "Adventures on the Wheels of Steel?"

The story unfolds while the fragments coalesce. I like to think of the kind of writing in *Rhythm Science* as script information – the self as "subject-in-synchronization" (the moving parts aligned in the viewfinder of an other), rather than the old twentieth-century inheritance of the Cartesian subject-object relation. What are the ontological implications for such a shift? What does this kind of "filmic time" do to the creative act, and how do we represent it? Film makers like Griffith, Dziga Vertov, Oscar Michaux, and Sergei Eisenstein were forging narratives for a world just coming out of the throes of World War I. The Soviet cinema's "dialectal montage" or "montage of attractions" created a kind of subjective intercutting of multiple layers of stories within stories. The post World War I world, like ours, was one that was becoming increasingly interconnected and filled with stories of distant lands, times, and places. It was a world where cross cutting allowed the presentation not only of parallel actions occurring simultaneously in separate spatial dimensions, but also of parallel actions occurring on separate temporal planes (in the case of Griffith's *Birth of a Nation*, four plot lines at once). These new cinematic strategies conveyed the sense of density that the world was confronting.

When jazz entered the pictures, the density of immersive narrative contexts inten-sified. Jazz time –versus- Hollywood time. Early films, like Oskar Fischinger's animated intro for Disney's *Fantasia* or Man Ray's shorts explored portray human subjects in relation to the objects around them. The first sound film to hit pop culture's criteria of mass sales and massive influence was Alan Crosland's 1927 epic *The Jazz Singer*. The ongoing relationship of how to flip between images arrives and conquers, becomes song. *The Jazz Singer* versus the silence of *Birth of a Nation* on the mind-screens of contemporary America: Echo meets alias in the coded exchange of glances. What Mikhail Bakhtin might have once called "diacritical difference" now becomes "the mix." Or, as James B. Twitchell says in *Adcult USA,* his classic analysis of advertising culture, media, and the "carnival of the everyday" in the images and sounds that make up the fabric of American daily life: "[The situations are] homologues of each other and semilogues of those in the genre. Entertainments share diachronic and synchronic similarities; they refer to individual texts as well as to all precursors and successors… every program-mer's worst fear is that we might change the channel. "

Compare that jazz-drenched cinematic flux to Dj mixes and see a similar logic at

work: The selection of sound becomes narrative. I guess that's traveling by synec-doche. It's a process of sifting through the narrative rubble of a phenomenon that conceptual artist Adrian Piper liked to call the "indexical present": "I use the notion of the 'indexical present' to describe the way in which I attempt to draw the viewer into a direct relationship with the work, to draw the viewer into a kind of self critical standpoint which encourages reflection on one's own responses to the work."

To name, to call, to upload, to download… So I'm sitting here and writing – creating a new time zone out of widely dispersed geographic regions – reflect and reflecting on the same ideas using the net to focus our attention on a world rapidly moving into what I like to call prosthetic realism. Sight and sound, sign and signification: The travel at this point becomes mental, and as with Griffith's hyper-dense technically prescient intercuts, it's all about how you play with the variables that creates the art piece. If you play, you get something out of the experience. If you don't, like Griffith – the medium becomes a reinforcement of what's already there, or as one critic, Iris Barry, said a long time ago of Griffith's *Intolerance*: "History itself seems to pour like a cataract across the screen."

any shift in
the traffic of
information
can create
not only new
thoughts, but
new ways of
thinking.

Like an acrobat drifting through the topologies of codes, glyphs, and signs that make up the fabric of my everyday life, I like to flip things around. With a culture based on stuff like Emergency Broadcast Network hyper-edited
new briefs, Ninja Tune dance moguls Cold Cut's "7 Minutes of Madness" remix of Eric B and Rakim's "Paid in Full" to Grandmaster Flash's "Adventures on the Wheels of Steel" to later excursions into geographic, cultural, and temporal dispersion like MP3lit.com, twenty-first-century aesthetics

needs to focus on how to cope with the immersion we experience on a daily level. Eisenstein spoke of this density back in 1929 when asked about travel and film: "The hieroglyphic language of the cinema is capable of expressing any concept, any idea of class, any political or tactical slogan, without recourse to the help of suspect dramatic or psychological past." Does this mean that we make our own films as we live them? Traveling without moving. It's something even Aristotle's Unmoved Mover wouldn't have thought possible. But hey, like I always say, "who's counting?"

So I'm sitting here at the airport, looking forward to a transfer in Frankfurt, and then a day flight back to NYC. I'll be there for a day, and then I'm off to Sweden and Denmark for four days. I just got "here" but the only real reason to be here is to go someplace else. I was in Brazil a day before, and I'm going to be traveling again. Back to NYC and the cycle starts over again. I look at my wrist-watch and check the time in several time zones, make a couple of phone calls to different people who I know are awake in the different geographic regions I need to deal with, and then try to pass the time by reading. I get on-line to check in on a couple different listservs that I subscribe to, and while it's all going I restart the CD player that I'm listening to go into "loop" mode 'cause hey, I don't feel like starting the damn thing over again. Is there any rhyme or reason to the whole situa-

tion? I look around at the airport's hustle and bustle, and it's lists of times, dates, and names all synchronized with the different departures and arrivals. Nothing is out of the ordinary. Nothing.

Panache – words and code modules, bits and bytes, temporal arbitrage. Follow the vector across a narrative arc and feel how the net's architecture resonates with the convergence of many cultures and styles. From math to code to culture, contemporary art has shifted as well. It all seems more and more that the creative act itself is becoming a source-code like Linux where people create and add modules of thought-ware to the mix, making it all a little more interesting. Speaking in code, we live in a world so utterly infused with digitality that it makes even the slightest action ripple across the collection of data bases we call the web. This is nothing new. Like one of my favorite artists – to

we live in a world so utterly infused with digitality that it makes even the slightest action ripple across the collection of data bases we call the web.

we live in a world so utterly infused with digitality that it makes even the slightest action ripple across the collection of data bases we call the web.

ERRATA ERRATUM

use the term in its metaphysical context – the physicist Richard P. Feynman, said, "The dream is to find the open channel. What, then is the meaning of it all? What can we say to dispel the mystery of existence? Admitting that we do not know and maintaining the attitude that we do not know the direction necessarily to go, permit the possibility of alteration, of thinking, of new contributions and new discoveries for the problem of developing a way to do what we want ultimately, even when we do not know what we want." Where from here?

Nets and bets, tasks a

Strange, inferential portraits of a seamlessly complex system for routing people and products, a system as intricate as a global nervous system without all the baggage... It all depends on your perspective. I'm at the airport waiting for my next flight. That's about as existential as you can get in these days of hyper-modernity. Cultural relativism – actually dealing with all the diversity out there – as I always like to say, from now to the beginning let it be like a record spinning. Nets and bets, tasks and masks, codes and modes, it all just flows. Do you get my drift?

Los Angeles' Museum of Contemporary Art (MOCA) commissioned me to do a piece for their on-line gallery. I decided to do a remix of Marcel Duchamp's *Sculpture Musical* and *Erratum Musical* works along the lines of a web-based Dj project because I thought it would be interesting to bring the issues of rhythm science to both art and a broader public, to reconcile of double and triple into multiplex consciousness through the lens of the historical avant-garde. The click of a mouse, the roll of a pair of dice – they both have a kind of intentionality behind them. One is directly relational, the other is lightly random. The art of Dj-ing rests somewhere in between those poles of chance. That valence is a kind of pendulum swing between how we can perceive something and why. The observer always alters the picture, the map always changes the routes traveled. There's always something to think through when you create a mix; that's why I was fascinated with Duchamp. There's an old story about why he stopped painting: He said simply that he had to "keep filling space in." Put simply, he was "into" the space between things, the motes of ideas and intentionality that objects and the emotions they invoke in us drifted through his mind like a self directed swarm of birds. The flocking instinct holds the geometry of the ideas together. Just like a flock of birds drifting in the empty skies of a Magritte painting. "Filling space in" becomes a dance with emptiness, and

that's what my *Errata Erratum* project was about. The remix and the original. The copy and the doppelganger. Who is who in a theater of sounds where any sound can be you? What relationships drift between the preconceptions of who is represented by what object or painting or sound? And always, the why?

The Duchamp response would be "Why not?"

The Duchamp remix was all about dub. I took a lot of his material written on music and flipped it into a Dj mix of his visual material – with him rhyming! Needless to say it was a fun project. So to give context here is important: there were no "finished" pieces and everything in *Errata Erratum* is about that gap between execution and intent in a world of uncertainty. Whatever mix you make of it, it can only be a guess - you have to make your own version, and that's kind of the point. With that in mind, I ask that you think of this as a mix lab - an "open system" where any voice can be you. The only limits are the game you play and how you play it.

During the time that I spent researching for *Errata Erratum*, I found so many examples of how Dj culture intersected with some of the core tenets of the twentieth-century avant-garde that it seems to have unconsciously absorbed them all.

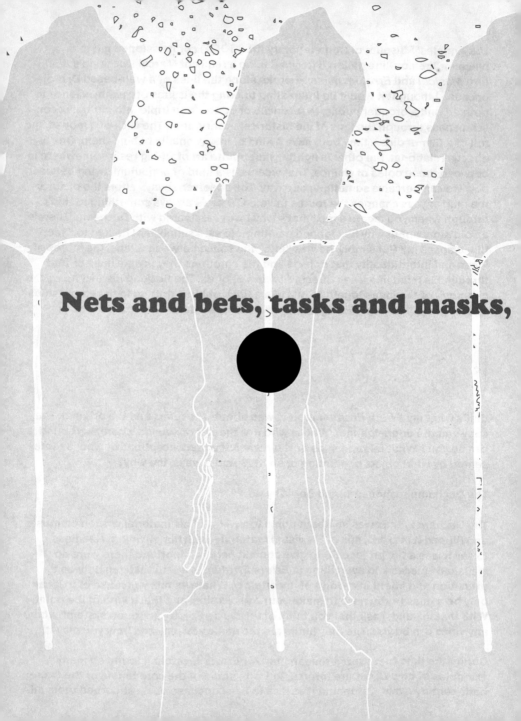

Nets and bets, tasks and masks,

codes and modes, it all just flows.

Composed in 1913, Duchamp's *Erratum Musical* is based on a whole schemata of mistakes, errors, and missteps in a family situation. What these days we'd call "glitches" in the programs's communication protocol, for him were a metaphysical critique of, as he put it so often, "how one can make a work of art that is not a work of art." For *Erratum Musical*, Duchamp wrote out a series of "instructions" for his sisters about the interaction of three sets of twenty-five cards. Each was to take a card from a hat passed around the room at the start and sing random phrases based on a loosely defined interpretation of the cards's patterned surfaces. Three voices in a trialogue formed the basis of the piece, with the cards little more than cues for the unconscious sonic impulses. Imagine a dinner party where people sing Rorshach ink blotter tunes, and you'll have a reasonable picture of what sounds the sisters came up with. It's not too Freudian a leap to think of these abstract voices as playing out familial dramas in sound... but hey, that's kind of the point. Dj-ing deals with extended kinship systems of rhythm — one beat matches or doesn't match a sound-flow, and it's the interpretation of the gestures that make up the mix that creates the atmosphere in a room. The *Errata Erratum* remix is a twenty-first-century update on the idea. But now, we move through dispersed networks of culture and the cards we play are icons on

a screen. In the remix, single notes are assigned not to playing cards, but rather to digitzed "roto-reliefs,"on-line representations of the engraved cards that Duchamp made throughout his career and gave away randomly to people.

The song became more dispersed as Duchamp became a better known artist. By the end of his life, the card game became a signature that was profoundly paradoxical. Like all of Duchamp's work it was personal and impersonal. *Errata Erratum* Dj-s "found objects" just like I would mix the records that normally comprise my sonic palette. *Errata Erratum* is an explicit experiment with sonic sculpture and the interplay of memory as it is shaped by the technologies of communication that have come to form the core conditions of daily life in the industrialized world. In short, it was meant to be a fun thing, and in short order it became something vastly more serious. Back the in the distant mid-nineties Dj-ing was still an underground phenomenon, and in a sense, today now that guitars are regularly outsold by turntables, the tables have literally turned. Dj-ing is a mainstream phenomenon, and mixing beats and sounds is a commonplace thing on the internet for kids. *Errata Erratum* is a migration of those values into a playful critique of one of the first artists to engage that logic of irreverence toward the art object and to apply that logic to some of the works that he came up with to flesh out his ideas on the topic in "net culture." When the circles move on the screen, they are explicitly referencing loops and repetition, cycles and flows, and the cyclic translation of one person's thoughts into another's. When the mix comes calling, you can't help but think of how many people are in it. This project is an attempt to bring together one of my favorite people in mix culture together with some variations on a certain theme – one that is as wide as the internet, and as wide as the people's thoughts moving through the fiber optic routing systems that hold our new version of the "digital sublime" together.

It's a milieu where each "musical sculpture" is unique yet completely dependent on the system that created the context. It's that old Duchamp paradox come back to haunt us, uncannily, on the internet. Duchamp said in his famous "Creative Act" lecture of 1957 (the recording of which comprises the "dub version" hip-hop track for my *Errata Erratum* remix), "all in all, the creative act is not performed by the artist alone; the spectator brings the work in contact with the external world by deciphering and interpreting its inner qualifications and thus adds his contribution to the creative act." Think of that as you hear Duchamp rhyming over a hip-hip dub rhythm I made specially for this project. Call him "M.C. Duchamp" because,

by hip-hop standards, he has good "flow." At this point in the track, his voice is separated from the recording to become part of the musical sculpture, and, like the original *Erratum Musical*, we're seeing someone's voice placed in a system of chance operations. Rhythm becomes the context for the performance and the artist becomes part of the sonic palette he describes.

For *Errata Erratum*, I wanted to streamline that process and give people a sense of improvisation. Like Duchamp, the pieces also indicate the instruments on which it should be performed, but they are icons made of digital code. Where he would write "player piano, mechanical organs or other new instruments for which the virtuoso intermediary is suppressed," we can click on a screen. The second part of his notes contained a description of the compositional system. The title for the "system" is: "An apparatus automatically recording fragmented musical periods." Here, again, we're left with the ability to make our own interpretation of a given framework, and are invited to run with it as a kind of game "system." The "apparatus" that let's you make the composition in his original notes is comprised of three parts: a funnel, several open-end cars, and a set of numbered balls. Think of all of them as being flattened out on your screen and that's what the *Errata Erratum* remix is about.

THE FUTURE IS HERE

I'm just happy to be alive in this era. It's truly exciting to travel around just checking out how strange it all is. I'd say this is going to be a century of hyper-acceleration, and I just get a kick out of seeing it. One of my favorite phrases comes from William Gibson: "The future is already here, it's just unevenly distributed."

So what is rhythm science and how do we measure its effects? A blip on the radar? A database sweep? A streamed numerical sequence? In a short space, my narrative has switched formats and functions, time and place – all were kind of like fonts – something to be used for a moment to highlight a certain mode of expression, and, of course, utterly pliable. As I sit here and type on my laptop, even the basic format of the words

I'm just happy to be alive in this era, just checking out how strang century of hyper-acceleration

I write still mirrors some of the early developments in graphical user interface-based texts still echoes not only in how I write, but how I think about the temporal placement of the words and ideas I'm thinking about. It is a worldview that definitely ain't linear. The likes of Alan Kay, Douglas Engelbert, and Ivan Sutherland pioneered graphical user interfaces more than three decades ago, allowing users to interact with the icons and objects on the monitor's surface. But what they accomplished was even more profound than that, their work lets us move into the screen world itself. Context becomes metatext, and the enframing process, as folks as diverse as Iannis Xenakis, Kool Keith a.k.a. Dr Octagon or Eminem can tell you, like media phiosopher Freidrich Kittler, "Aesthetics begins as 'pattern recognition.'"

We're probably the first generation to grow up in a completely electronic environment. I always think about the first time John Cage went into an "anechoic
chamber," a place where there is literally "no sound" and he heard two weird
rhythm patterns: one high frequency and one low frequency. The low frequency
pattern was the sound of his blood circulating in his veins, and the high frequency
was the sound of his nervous system. These days we'd be able to emulate and
precisely take the sound of someone's "operating system" – wetware and hardware – and simulate them from the ground up. Once you get their basic credit
information and various electronic representations of that person, who needs
the real thing anymore? That's one of the oppositions I explore: my art critiques
live and non-live. The two are utterly mutually conditioning, and this cycle will
only intensify throughout the twenty-first century.

Repetition and Claude Shannon? Repetition and James Snead? As has been
well documented by folks such as Tricia Rose and Sherry Turkle (whose book
The Second Self is itself a digital era update on Du Bois's double consciousness)
the sense here is one of prolonging the formal implications of the expressive act.
Move into the frame, get the picture, re-invent your name. Movement, flow, flux:

... It's truly exciting to travel around
get it all is. I'd say this is going to be a
and I just get a kick out of seeing it

the nomad takes on the sedentary qualities of the urban dweller. Movement
on the screen becomes an omnipresent quality. Absolute time becomes dream
machine flicker. The eyes move. The body stays still. Travel. Big picture small
frame, so what's the name of the game? All at once, the digital codes becomes
symbol and synecdoche, sign and signification.

Sometimes stories work better.

First Story: One of the more intriguing parties I've been to was a few years ago
just outside of Reykjavik. The mostly Icelandic crowd was rocking out. People
were on glaciers, on the snow, in the cold, and the sound and light systems were
also outside, scattered on the ice fields. It was dark, a surreal, gray dawn. The
crowd was into hard techno and trance. In Iceland, there is a mix of cultures –
Scandinavian, Inuit, and European – and they are also just a really open and
friendly people, a fishing culture, a small island. When I got back from that party,
I cut all my hair off, leaving green, foot long dreads on the floor.

Second Story: I was living at the Gas Station on Avenue B in Alphabet City on
Manhatttan's Lower East Side. I used to throw after hours-parties, we'd just leave

I'm just happy to be alive in this era. It's truly exciting to travel around just checking out how strange it all is. I'd say this is going to be a century of hyper-acceleration, and I just get a kick out of seeing it.

the door open, and homeless people, crazy people would come through. For one party we put up these TVs, and every TV had static, and they were hanging from these industrial chains on the ceiling. People were coming in off the street, I had no idea who the fuck they were, but they would jump onto the TVs and swing around. The televisions were the only light in the room, and there was crazy music, and then you'd look out and see the melted metal and burned up sculptures. But that was a different time.

Third Story: It was one of those strange evenings that are becoming more and more quotidian in the twenty-first century. It was the middle of summer and a concert of Iron Maiden and Queensryche – two towering icons of seventies and eighties arena rock that some call heavy metal, and others just call plain old rock and roll – had just finished. I was sitting in the back of a taxi in a traffic jam caused by crowds exiting Madison Square Garden, summer heat adding layers and layers of "body noise" to the heady mix of the people swirling through the stalled cars and pointillist rendered signs blinking down on the snarled currents of humanity flowing through New York's center, I decided to simply let my mind float and go nowhere fast. I was presented with something that contemporary

America seems to have in abundance, and that other countries are struggling to catch up with – a trend I like to call "demographic nostalgia." Each part of the crowd reflected their appreciation of the bands they had come to see. Stuck in the traffic their migration from the arena was causing, I was given a great point of view on the migratory patterns of the gathered concert-goers. They left the Garden and moved from the finely tuned precision of rows and seat numbers into clumps and clusters of people held together only by fashion and previous social and geographic allegiance like so many particles of gas drawn together by electro-chemical valences and atomic mass. The rules of the "real" world were asserting themselves and the crowd heeded the call of natural selection, twenty-first-century style.

Fourth Story: I was in Tokyo and doing a show with an old Japanese friend of mine, Dj Krush, and some new folks on the block, Anticon, young white kids from Middle America. They were doing a collaboration with Krush, a piece called "Song for John Walker" – the suburban kid who joined the Taliban. Needless to say, the backstage vibe was all about dialogue and we were all just kicking it. Krush's wife walked in and handed him a samurai sword before his set, and everyone in the room was... ummm... kind of silent. In a moment like that, the strangeness (strange-mess) of global culture, hip-hop, and of operating as a DJ on a global level crystallized before my eyes. We all sat there and paused for a second. It really felt like a still from a video art installation. Krush doesn't speak English, and we have communicated mostly with beats over the years. The show was a benefit for Afghani war orphans at Tokyo's Liquid Room in the Shinjuku district, and well... you just had to feel the oddity of being in a room with some white Americans talking about a lawyer's kid who read Malcolm X and defected to a terrorist organization and a Japanese

DEMOGRAPHIC NOSTALGIA

kid who prayed with his family and was into Shinto Buddhism chants before he went on stage to do turntable tricks. A scene like that doesn't fit into any normal categorization of hip-hop that normal America wants, and it never will. That's the joy of being able to see how this stuff is unfolding in a real way across the globe. It's almost exactly a social approximation of the way web culture collapses distinctions between geography and expression, and it's almost as if the main issues of the day are all about how people are adjusting to the peculiarity of being in a simultaneous yet unevenly distributed world.

THE PROSTITUTE

You are alone in a garden of memory in an Eden with no script and no temptation. The apple of knowledge is an ad on a website somewhere. Enter keyword "truth," and the search engine brings you conflicting meanings. That's the prostitute's revenge: so many people, so little time. In the network, you can't take a bite. The prostitute in the conveyor belt. It's a simple metaphor. The prostitute in the factory. It's a simpler one. In both cases you must realize that it's not about a person, but the locus of intent and the negative dialectics of a role-playing game where your demands of a person are based just as much on their willingness to play a role as on the basic fact that the money being handed over is an emblem of your time and energy. It's a dance contest between master and slave, but again, and maybe, just maybe, it might possess you. It's a voodoo economics of the information

always try to create one new scenarios aliznos moment of flight. ho

era. You pay the price and expect to receive satis-faction. Think of it as a Taylorization of urban pattern recognition: that sense of wandering through an indeterminate maze of intentionality is what makes up the creative act – selection and detection, morphology of structure. Yes, dialectical triangulation, suspension of disbelief. It's all down by law. Those are what make the new art go round. The prostitute knows this. Again and again – that refrain – software, wetware, shareware, hardware; the prostitute has carnal knowledge of them all.

The music and art I create is an end result of a life lived in an environment where almost all aspects of urban life were circumscribed by the coded terrains of a planet put in parentheses by satellites in the sky beaming back everything long ago. The conflict of African and European cultural patterns, the uncertainty of origin that marks all life in the United

States, the sense of living in a racially divided culture that has lost the ability to really think about anything but media entertainment – these issues act as a kind of formative crucible for anyone who is still idealistic. I don't know of any artist who really thinks everything is locked down. Things can change. Here's the deal – Situationist style generative psychogeography – jumping from topic to topic, culture to culture, website to website, thought to thought, becomes rhyme time – we're looking at a life lived in a tapestry woven of words and the beats that give them cadence. I flip the script and float. The prostitute scenario is about an end of definitions – breaking the loops, and watching the role collapse in on itself when it's no longer occupied. Kind of like watching an empty husk sink in on itself after everything has been sucked out of it.

Chastity, like skepticism, shouldn't be relinquished too readily, and that's what the sampler tells us. Play with the recognizeability of texts and see what happens. Pay the piper, and call the tune. Advertising is the modern substitute for argument; its function is to make the worse appear the better. Both advertising and argument have ideal extensions that lend utility to their conditions. Nothing is really so poor and melancholy as art that is interested in itself and not in its

subject. The truth is cruel, but it can be loved, and it makes free those who have loved it.

My challenge to myself is to always try to create new worlds, new scenarios at almost every moment of thought. The transactions I speak of take me outside of the normal cash flow of role playing because it's multiple. Into the picture, into the frame – that's the name of the game. It's a dance of measured steps at the production line, and of course, we're talking about the oldest profession here. In a society based on spectacle, it's about seeing what images and sounds coerce you into certain behavior patterns, and again and again, the abstract image of the prostitute beckons.

Pay the piper and call the tune. It's a mark of a production process that produces an intangible result that's both personal and impersonal. For me it's really coming down to the way you can braid your own personal narrative with the multiplex consciousness notion, the development of sonic sculpture as a way to meld music and art, and the stresses brought about by trying to blend mass entertainment with what used to be thought of as high culture. In the meantime and in-between time, like the old song says, "I don't mean to brag, I don't mean to boast, but I like

hot butter on a breakfast toast." Catch the beat, rock the spot. The multiplex concept of the self seems key if you want to avoid the context – that's the idea of the screen-saver self. When your attention is unoccupied, someone else takes your place. You wear a sign saying "hello, I'm not here right now."

The Prostitute. The oldest profession. This character is one who will end the narrative, and pass your gaze back to the idiot who started the loop cycle. Think of a scenario where you pay and or someone pays you; it's a computational dialectic, a micropolitics of loops (again). The role of the prostitute plays on your mind like an invisible hand that caresses your electromagnetic memories. Messages need to be delivered, codes need to be interpreted, and information, always, is hungry for new routes to move through. That's the agency thing, that's the prostitute's role. The stripper takes off her clothes to put on her audience, the prosti-tute looks at you and says, "Who do you want me to be?" It's a mime dance, a pantomime of desire and projection. It's a dyslexic

shuffle of autopoesis between two undercover agents who carry their orders clutched in dead hands - the transfer of information between them is an Interrelationship between music and art and writing. I guess that's what the subliminal seduction scenario creates - a dialectical triangulation between thesis, anti-thesis, synthesis. The paradox here is that you have a culture founded on unceasing change and transformation - so much so that things change to quickly that there's no there there - the agency of change is a dead end without ceaseless transformation, and that's where music and philosophy intersect. If architecture is nothing but frozen music, philosophy is the music that forms the sound track of this transaction. Yeah, no doubt it's about that blending and blurring of the whole subject-object scenario, that Cartesian dualism of doubt imploded on itself, the mind and body rendered as cultural critique of a multiplex mind. Think of it as dematerialized sculpture. Again, the prostitute asks, "What do you want from me?"

Have I spoken around the topic too much? That's kind of the point. Nothing is direct, everything is an interpretation. I'm just following the patterns that I use to think about things. So again: Think of the actions of customer and prostitute as corporate transactional realism – projection, interrogation, fragmentation. It's all about looking for solace in the arms of someone remote from your experiences, someone who evokes a different memory. Think of it as sublimation seeking solace in the arms of alienation. It's the oldest profession, and that's what brings us to the breakdown. This is not a critique of cynical reason. Map one metaphor onto another, check the vibe, and create a new pattern. That's what I ask: Break the loops. Transactional realism: It's an old sampling of tone form again and again – sampling as a mode of creation, a way of dealing with overflow, of internalizing the machinery of collective culture. But the danger within writing, of taking sampling too far – too much citation, not enough synthesis – leads to the break with the old form. Who speaks through you? Sound creates a way of thinking about these issues in a way that the visual and the narrative flow into that rupture in the system of seduction. It perfects and popularizes before the other arts even adopt to the changed conditions. That's what the transactional reality reminds you: This is not a polite situation.

You can never play a record the same way for the same crowd. That's why remixes happen. Memory demands newness. You have to always update your archive. "Act global, think local." This is what Dj-ing tells us in the era of the sample. The sample is an interrogation of the meaning we see in a song, of its emotional content lifted away like a shroud from a dead corpse, only to be refitted and placed on another body. That's the deal – you renew the cloth by repurposing the fabric. That's recycling. The world of sounds is a context buster. Local can just be the thought patterns bouncing around in your head at the moment or the radio that you're able to get in a certain geographic area. It can also be stuff that you receive from the Internet. The options are almost infinite in terms of sound construction. The best way would be to implode and see what's inside.

End:
At the end of the day, as the final words flow across the screen, and the book comes to an end, just think of the abstract image of the prostitute in the assembly line, the mix speaks through you and disrupts the flow of the spectacle in your mind. Just hum this line to yourself as you flip the script. You're only buggin'.

AUTHOR'S ACKNOWLEDGEMENTS

There's an old adage that I think about whenever I write: "Make the people think that they think, and they love you. Actually make them think, and they hate you." It's been an uphill struggle over the last several years to create some kind of context for a different perspective on Dj culture, and the list of people I would like to thank for their support over the years stretches between really old acquaintances and

new folks whom I've met along the way. The path to knowledge doesn't really have an end, you just realize that the road keeps going, and everything – information, the social networks that provide structure and sustain your inquiry into whatever you're investigating – well, each is just a stop along the way. At the end of the day, it's all about people. First and foremost I'd like to dedicate this book to my mother for her patience with a sometimes quite hyper child, and my sister and her family: the Millers are a growing clan, and we all need to see each other grow and transform in these times. I love you all and yeah, I wish Dad were here to read this new book. The book is an echo of his memory as well.

Then there are the friends and allies who have helped over the years – we are a community of sound reflecting a unity we've unexpectedly found: Beth Coleman, Howard Goldkrand, Enrique Candioti, Ken Jordan, Tamara Palmer, Kodwo Eshun, Erik Davis, Ishmael Reed, Manuel De Landa, Vivek Bald, David Goldberg, Roy Christopher, Doug Rushkoff, Samuel Delaney, Roselee Goldberg, Donald Ododita, Sussan Deyhim, Steve Cohen, John S. Johnson, William Clark, Cay Rabinowitz, Shahzia Sikander, Mariko Mori, Shirin Neshat, Mad Professor, Dan Yashiv, George Condo, Peter Halley, Ibrahim Quirashi, Talvin Singh, Peter Fleisig, Peter Lunenfeld, Eve Mcsweeney, Julian Laverdiere, Aenoch, Seth Fershko, Tara Rodgers (Pink Noise crew!), Ashley Crawford, High Priest, Matthew Shipp, William Parker, Pauline Oliveros, Steve Reich, Meredith Monk, Iannis Xenakis, Kut Masta Kurt, Ari Marcopoulos, Diego Cortez, Karsh Kale, Dj Rekha, Andrea Parker, Robin Rimbaud a.k.a. Scanner, Steven Shaviro, Charles Mudede,

Farai Chideya, Akin Adams... and if there are people that I've forgotten somehow, hey... you know how it goes.

This book is a reflection of the many conversations I've had with you all, and hopefully you'll see the paths of change that have echoed through our dialogues as we have all transformed, and gone deeper and deeper into the mix. Thanx for the support over the years.

peace at you all!

and remember – as George Clinton said so many years ago:

Think! It ain't illegal yet!

Paul D. Miller

Think! It ain't illegal yet!

You can never play a record the same way for the same crowd. That's why remixes happen. Memory demands newness. You have to always update your archive. "Act global, think local." This is what Dj-ing tells us in the era of the sample.

DESIGNERS' NOTES

We've sampled the sampler. This project has been a lesson in translation and the art of the Dj. A Dj makes an entirely new thing out of other things, be it rhythm or word, and so our approach to this book was to work with the images, ideas, and music that Paul gave us and to deliver something as much us as him, as much assembled as brand new, a translation of his thoughts, images, and rhythms into our medium. Our work is based on the clear presentation of concepts through design; all of our decisions come from the content before us.

The look of the thing you're holding is derived from the requirements of the book series and Paul's own needs. As Paul has an A side and a B side on his 12" records and in this book, so the paper the book's printed on is two sided: rough and slick, each containing its own pleas- ures. We had to hold a CD (our own C side to the book) but we didn't want to hide it—we believe in transparency. So we decided to both emphasize it physically and to deploy it as a conceptual tool. The button used to hold the disc appears as a hole in the cover and then through the entire book—an uninterrupted depth in the middle of an otherwise solid object. Music, like the space, goes on and on, but both also disrupt and disturb. The button is embedded in that ever-shifting circular form which revolves as you read, perhaps as a mute soundtrack or simply foreshadowing the one soon to play out loud. In the end, it's the physical disc itself, and its form is derived from Paul's visuals, as are many other vector graphics in the book. They can be read as text, or indeed, as one reads graffiti on a wall. And like a record, we designed this book for progressive, though flexible, motion. Vectors (and their graphics) connect the turning pages as much as the type does. This book can be read chapter-by-chapter, digested via the text-bites, or scanned through the images; you, dear reader, can now sample us.

We'd like to thank Paul D. Miller, for his work and support. And very special thanks to Peter Lunenfeld for giving us the room to do what we do. Without his ample encouragement and free approach to design and content, this book wouldn't have been possible.

Cornelia Blatter and Marcel Hermans, COMA.

ENDTRODUCTION

GIVE
ME
TWO
RNTABLES,
AND
I'LL
MAKE
YOU
A
UNIVERSE.

One, that's just a singularity. Two, well, with two, you can make a line. But three, now there's something you can work with. Three lets you define a plane, a space, a vector. I'm starting with points here, and good old-fashioned Euclidean geometry, but I could just as easily be talking about words or images or sounds. *Rhythm Science* is the third pamphlet in the Mediawork series, and as such it serves to fully materialize the point developed with *Utopian Entrepreneur* (2001), and the line drawn between it and *Writing Machines* (2002). *Rhythm Science* doesn't just help to place the series, it also opens a shared space for words, images, and sounds.

Many artists and intellectuals want the freedom to move between fields and forms, but few of them are able to create equally well and with equivalent

passion across disciplines. Paul D. Miller aka Dj Spooky that Subliminal Kid can and does. Fusion is central to his work. He melds jazz with rap, performance with theory, art with pop culture. His non-stop performances give him a global worldview, but do not remove Paul from what he sees as his roots in the American side of the African Atlantic. In *Rhythm Science*, Paul lays out aesthetic strategies for an era of multiplex con-sciousness. Rhythm is central, not only because music holds such ancient command over our very selves, but also because sound technologies so often set the pattern for other cultural movements (think of the way that both sampling and file sharing achieved cultural prominence far earlier in music than in video). Every project Paul engages with is part of a process. He wants to convey a sense of how conceptual art, popular culture, and idealism can function in this day and age. It is so important to have artists and thinkers who imagine a better world, who stake their claim on a future that breaks the trap of *Blade Runner*-style pessimism. To use his own, distinct vocabulary, Paul is actionary, not re-actionary.

At one point in the development of this project, Paul and I spent some time together in the Mojave Desert. All through that week, I kept thinking of something that he said a decade before: Give me two turntables, and I'll make you a universe. To design this book, I wasn't looking just for someone to give form to the words, though that's important. I wanted someone who would follow Paul into the realm of universe-making. Rather than one, I found two universe-makers in COMA, the redoubtable team of Cornelia Blatter (the CO) and Marcel Hermans (the MA). Together they are an innovative, interdisciplinary art and design studio that maintains offices on two continents. They conceptualize, art direct, design, and produce work in various media from print to Internet to environments. Recent projects include the 2003 *365: AIGA Year in Design*, *Architectural Laboratories: Greg Lynn & Hani Rashid* (NAi), art direction and design for *FRAME* magazine, and the redesign of *Index* magazine. Multiple winners of the AIGA 50 books/50 covers award, they have also won an *I.D.* Design Review. With *Rhythm Science*,

they have crafted a living, breathing space for words, images, and sounds, and have transcended even my expectations of how seductive a theoretical fetish object can be.

Major ongoing funding for the *Mediawork Pamphlet* series comes from the Rockefeller Foundation. The first three Pamphlets benefited from a start-up grant from Jeffrey and Catharine Soros. Additional funding provided by the Office of the President, Art Center College of Design. Guy-Marc Hinant of Sub Rosa records in Belgium cannot be thanked enough for allowing us to include the CD with this volume. Thanks also to: Steve Cohen of Music and Art Management, Inc; Brenda Laurel, Anne Burdick and Philip van Allen, my colleagues from Art Center's graduate Media Design Program; Peter Halley, and Joshua Trees & Yvan Martinez of Fake ID for the *Rhythm Science* WebTake at mitpress.mit.edu/mediawork. Finally, the unwavering enthusiasm of Doug Sery, from the MIT Press, is matched only by the quality of his input.

Peter Lunenfeld
Editorial Director, Mediawork Pamphlet Series

**GIVE
ME
TWO
TURNTABLES,
AND
I'LL
MAKE
YOU
A
UNIVERSE.**

A Mediawork Pamphlet
mitpress.mit.edu/mediawork

© 2004 Paul D. Miller

*Rhythm Science: Excerpts and Allegories
from the Sub Rosa Archives* audio CD
courtesy Guy-Marc Hinant, Sub Rosa
Brussels, Belgium. www.subrosa.net

Production by
COMA Amsterdam/New York

Printed and bound by
robstolk®, The Netherlands

Library of Congress
Cataloging-in-Publication Data

Dj Spooky That Subliminal Kid.
  Rhythm Science / Paul D. Miller.
    p. cm.—(Mediawork pamphlets)
  ISBN 0-262-63287-X (pbk. : alk.paper)
  1. Technology and civilization. 2. Science
  and civilization. 1. Title. II. Mediawork.

CB478.D5 2004
303.48'3—dc22   2003061503

10 9 8 7 6 5 4

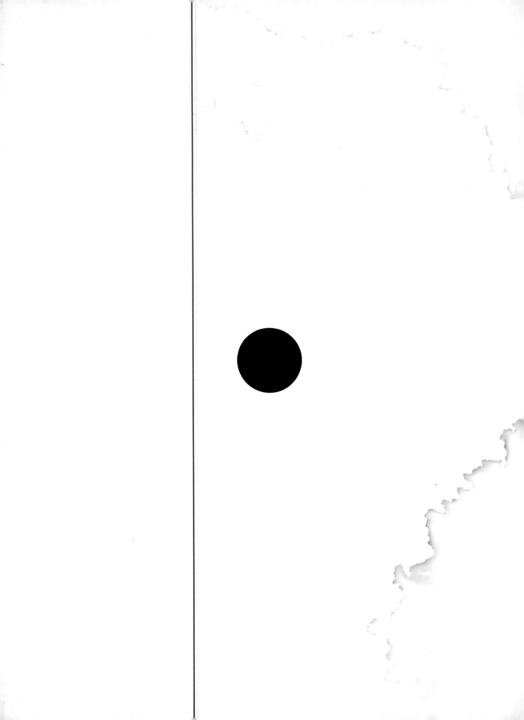